AF303880

Also by Gino Leineweber

Immersion in the Dhamma
My Experiences with an American Buddhist Monk

Hello Darkness, Poems 2010 – 2014
When Love is Guiding You, Poems 2015 – 2018
Everything is True, Poems 2019 – 2022

GINO LEINEWEBER

HEMINGWAY
HOW IT ALL BEGAN

CHILDHOOD AND YOUTH IN MICHIGAN

VERLAG EXPEDITIONEN

© Verlag Expeditionen,
Hamburg, Germany 2024

Gino Leineweber
Hemingway – How it all began
Childhood and Youth in Michigan
2. Edition

Cover design
Angela Schwarze, Berlin, Germany
Graphics in book
Lucio Ronca, Vietri sul Mare, Italy
Author's portrait
Katja Dietermann, Hamburg, Germany

ISBN: 978-3-911320-04-7

In memoriam
of my father

Biography

Gino Leineweber, born in 1944, has been a prominent figure in the literary world for over two decades as a poet, writer, and translator, and his leadership skills have been shown through his twelve-year tenure as the head of the Hamburg Authors' Association (HAV). His exceptional leadership was acknowledged in 2015 when he was appointed as honorary chairman.

From 2013 to 2020, Gino Leineweber's leadership was instrumental as he was president of the Three Seas Writers' and Translators' Council (TSWTC), based in Rhodes, Greece. He is currently a board member of the PEN Center German-Speaking Authors Abroad (formerly German Exile PEN).

Gino Leineweber's literary prowess extends beyond borders. He is a published author of travel writing, biographies, and poetry, with his poetic works resonating in numerous languages and earning him prestigious international awards. His linguistic versatility is evident as he writes in German and American English, and since 2016, he has also been translating prose and poetry from English.

He lives in Hamburg, Germany and Vietri sul Mare, Italy.

Notes and Acknowledgements

I am delighted that the English edition of Ernest Hemingway's biography—his childhood and early youth as I see it—is now in a completely revised new edition ten years after the first release stands available. When I first visited Michigan in 2008, I discovered that Hemingway spent much time in these places during his childhood and early youth. He began to write there and celebrated his first wedding in the small village of Horton Bay.

The connection between the locations and the literary genius of Hemingway encouraged my curiosity and propelled me to delve deeper into his biography. As I embarked on this journey, I realized that not only the German literature on Hemingway barely scratched the surface of this pivotal phase of his writing career. I traced his footsteps to the places that shaped his childhood and youth, the settings he immortalized in his stories. This personal exploration enriched my understanding of Hemingway, both as a writer and as a person.

Investing my time and energy in learning about this great writer's life has been very rewarding. I was lucky to meet wonderful people who were crucial to my research and who helped me in any way they could.

I want to extend my heartfelt gratitude to James Vol Fox (†) and Bob (Robert) Metzger from Horton Bay, whose insights and hospitality were invaluable to my research. I am also deeply thankful to the writer Michael Federspiel and the journalist Liz (Elizabeth) Edwards of Traverse Magazine for their support and encouragement.

The sources that I used I have indicated in the text. I took all quotes from Hemingway's letters, as not otherwise noted, from *Hemingway-Selected Letters 1917–1961* by Carlos Baker.

Gino Leineweber
June 2024

Gino Leineweber

Hemingway
How it all began

Childhood and Youth in Michigan

Chapter 1

Understanding how and why Hemingway was such a gifted author is the best approach to exploring his childhood and youth. Focusing solely on his life as an adult, his adventurous deep-sea fishing expeditions, African safaris, and his passion for boxing would be relatively unproductive.

To fully grasp the source and strength of Hemingway's literary gifts, one must trace him back to "Windemere" on Walloon Lake in Northern Michigan. Confine him to Cuba, Key West in Florida, or even the civil war in Spain as the essential locations in his life, missing out on the one place that had the most significant influence on his creative life.

To truly understand the growth of literary qualities in the young Ernest Hemingway, it is necessary to lay aside the tales of his legendary obsessive drinking, macho womanizing, or love of boxing and bullfighting. One must experience him in Horton Bay or Petoskey, where he could be found on excursions to lakes and creeks with his friend Bill or in a hammock, reading a book. Or where he could be imagined swimming in a lake on warm summer days, feeling breezes through the spruce as he walked barefoot through the woods, rowing out on a lake in the evening sun, wandering the hills, or fishing for trout in Horton Creek. Here lies the root, source, and strength of his literary vocation.

In the book *Hemingway in Michigan*, biographer Constance Cappel compared him to a 'migratory bird' that returned each summer to spend his vacation 'Up in Michigan.'

Here, he discovered and nurtured his calling as a writer. Here, he gathered himself, created an independent personality, and learned to fish, hunt, drink, and meet girls. Here, he learned to focus and take his writing seriously.

Hemingway grew up in a relatively puritanical home. His father, Dr. Clarence Edmond Hemingway, known as Ed, was a physician in Oak Park, a suburb of Chicago. Today, the Hemingway house on 339 N. Oak Park is home to The Ernest Hemingway Foundation and open to visitors. Another Hemingway home, from 1906 and also in Oak Park, is now in private hands. In 1896, Dr. Hemingway married Grace Hall, a woman of an artistic disposition from a wealthy Chicago family who had wished to become an opera singer. Ed was a sporty, outdoor man who enjoyed fishing and hunting, whereas Grace's interests lay more in Chicago society and artistic pursuits.

Hemingway had four sisters and was his parents' only son until his sixteenth year, when, as the last sibling, his brother Lester was born. Ernest, the second child, did not have a good relationship with his parents, for whom "good and evil" were clearly defined and what they insisted on. His father severely punished his son for any deviation.

Card games and dancing were prohibited, and Sunday church attendance was duty-bound for all family members. The boy grew into a powerful and energetic young man continually striving to escape the choking provincial shackles of his home, determined to write and not to accept the world as it was.

In the autumn of 1917, the time came for Ernest Hemingway, born July 21, 1899, to leave home. He withstood his parent's wish for him to go to college after high school. Instead, his uncle and father's brother, Tyler, intervened, securing him a post as a reporter with *The Kansas City Star*. America drew into The First

World War, and Ernest volunteered. When a colleague at the Star brought his attention to The Red Cross Ambulance Corps, he applied and was accepted. Towards the end of 1918, Ernest left Kansas with his friend, Carl Edgar, and two companions, setting out for a fishing holiday in Michigan. Here, he received a telegram informing him that he had set sail for Europe from New York on May 8.

The young Hemingway was confronted with war and found his place and recognition in this warlike situation. As Second Lieutenant in the ambulance service, he was proud to be photographed in his decorated US Army officer's uniform.

However, it would appear that being just an ambulance corps officer was not enough for his public image, as seen from photos where he had removed his Red Cross badge from his uniform.

In 1918, he crossed the Atlantic in a French liner named after Chicago, his hometown. Deployed in Northern Italy, at the foot of the Dolomites, he was an ambulance driver with tasks of transporting the wounded from the hillsides to the field hospitals down below. He even volunteered to take cigarettes and chocolate by bicycle twice daily to soldiers on the Front.

On one of these occasions, a soldier was killed, and Hemingway and several others were seriously injured when a hand grenade exploded in their midst.

Later, the Italian Government decorated Hemingway with the *Silver Medal for Bravery*.

Included in his certificate of bravery was, among other things: "Ernest Miller Hemingway ... responsible for carrying sundries (articles of comfort) to the Italian troops engaged in combat, gave proof of courage and self-sacrifice. Gravely wounded … with an admirable spirit of brotherhood before taking care of himself, he rendered generous assistance to the Italian soldiers more seriously injured by the same explosion and did not allow himself to be carried elsewhere until after they had been evacuated … "

On June 16, 1918, in a letter to his family from his sickbed, Hemingway wrote: "The 227 wounds I got from the trench mortar didn't hurt a bit at the time; only my feet felt like I had rubber boots full of water on. Hot water. And my knee cap was acting queer. The machine gun bullet just felt like a sharp smack on my leg with an icy snow ball. However, it spilled me. But I got up again and got my wounded into the dug out. I kind of collapsed at the dug out."

On his return to the United States, Hemingway visited his much-loved Michigan, where he had spent considerable time every summer since birth, enjoying many carefree vacations. Michigan, a state of unique geographical features, is surrounded by four of the five Great Lakes in North America: Lake Erie, Lake Huron,

Lake Michigan, and Lake Superior, the world's largest freshwater lake. The name Michigan is derived from the Indian word Mishigami and roughly means 'great lake,' which is no exaggeration. The given term Great Lakes State is proper because more than half of the state consists of the Great Lakes and numerous smaller ones. No state resident must travel more than six miles to a lake. However, what truly sets Michigan apart is its geographical division into two distinct parts: the Upper Peninsula and the Lower Peninsula.

The main occupational activities in the northern part of the Lower Peninsula and the Upper Peninsula were tree felling, fur trading, and fishing. These practices ceased at the turn of the twentieth century, paving the way for a thriving tourism industry. Although if I can entirely ignore mass tourism signs such as those on Mackinac Island, I cannot say severe damage to the landscape is evident. Tourism here is mainly individual and leaves minor or non-lasting damage.

Michigan has the most significant number of National Parks in the United States. However, its greatest fame comes from Detroit's city—the hub of the car automobile industry. It is situated in the Lower Peninsula's extreme southeast corner, whereas tracing Hemingway leads northwest and to the Upper Peninsula.

From 1898, the Hemingway family spent their vacations here, first with their then-only daughter,

Marceline, and later with all their up to six children. They were captivated by the magic of Northern Michigan among undulating hills, lakes, and forests. Here, they would remain undisturbed for the duration of the school vacation.

Dr. Hemingway could not always be with the family due to the pressures of work and the need to earn a living.

Their first visit took them by the beauty of the countryside around Walloon Lake—then called Bear Lake—that they looked around for land to build a holiday home. Henry Bacon, later called "Grandpa Bacon" by the children, provided them with what they were after 4,000 square meters of land on a lake shore where they could spend their vacation. They built a simple, structurally sound cottage with a large fireplace in the living room; an oil lamp gave light for reading and piano playing. As the years passed, they gradually extended it and made an outhouse in the little pine forest at the house's back. The house was surrounded by a spring well, from where they pumped water by hand and birch, cedar, oak, and beech trees. Grace baptized it Windemere after a lake in England. The southwest veranda provided a good view of the lake, and the parents could keep an eye on their children.

There was a little sandy strand, and they would swim and wash their clothes in the lake's blue water. The family lived their life in and around the water. It was a constant source of fun and entertainment.

Dr. Hemingway spent much time with his children, teaching them swimming, including lifesaving maneuvers. He drilled them in these techniques and even organized swimming competitions to ensure the children could compete in their disciplines. Over the years, the family had watercraft of all kinds, from rowing boats and canoes to their first motorboat in 1910. In a different context, Marjorie Bump, a friend and playmate of the children, had the following to say:

> Dr. Hemingway was a wonderful man who was easy to love. He had eyes like the softest cashmere, with kindness buried in their depths. One stormy night, he had to be tough and scold us after our nighttime lark of going out canoeing on Walloon Lake without permission. Even then, his eyes were expressively kind and tender, though his strong disapproval reminded us that we had not been safe.

Furthermore, under their father's guidance, the children learned about fishing. Dozens of family photos with trout, pike, and perch bear graphic witness to the success of his instruction and the bounty of the inland lakes at that time. The shooting was an integral part of the Hemingway family vacations as well. Skeet shooting was central to Sunday afternoon activities. They did not shoot for fun; hunting was also a leisure activity. However, Dr. Hemingway's explicit instructions to his children were they could not kill an animal if it could not eaten by them later.

Windemere was an open house for guests and special festivities. Family members, including grandparents and friends, came for extended visits, like barbecues on the Fourth of July. In 1911, their daughter Carol was born in Windemere. The fun and freedom the children enjoyed at the cottage were in no way curtailed by their having to contribute to the duties and responsibilities involved in the daily running and upkeep of the house.

Despite the idyllic vacations, Hemingway felt lost and misunderstood in this family dynamic with an overbearing mother and a weak father. On the other hand, I imagine him as enriched, forgetting the world and finding pleasure in the woods and lakes of Michigan, where he could fish and hunt beyond the confines of his life in Chicago. In his book Ernest Hemingway on Writing, had nothing positive to report on his upbringing:

Question: What is the best early training for a writer?
Hemingway: An unhappy childhood.

Chapter 2

His experiences in Michigan greatly influenced him and became part of his writing. In his younger years, 1916 and 1917, Hemingway wrote his first three short stories published in the school journal Tabula. Corresponding to the notion that a writer can only write his experiences, the young Hemingway began shaping stories about people and places he knew and understood in Michigan.

In the story Judgment of Manitou (he uses the Ottawa Indian word Manitou for God), the picture fits when he writes about nature and violence. A conflict between two men near the Canadian border ends deadly. The two trappers, Dick and Pierre, are the main characters in this short story. Pierre has become suspicious of Dick, thinking that he has taken his lost wallet. So, he sets a snare trap for Dick when he goes out to check his bear trap. Dick is soon caught and hangs from a tree to meet his fate, hence, being eaten by timber wolves. Pierre soon realizes that it was a red squirrel that stole his wallet. He rushes out to find what's left of Dick and is then caught by Dick's bear trap to face the 'Judgment of Manitou.'

The second story, The Matter of Color, is more of an anecdote than a short story. There is no plot or dramatic build-up. It is about a fight between two boxers, a white man, Montana Dan Morgan, and a black man, Joe Gans. Dan has injured his punching hand. Although he cannot use it, he takes part in the fight. Beforehand, however, he pays a big Swede to hit Joe on the head from hiding behind the curtain next to the ring. But the Swede knocks Dan out instead. He hit the wrong man because he is colorblind.

In the third story, Sepi Jingan, there is contact, for the first time, with an actual person, the Indian Billy Tabeshaw, who would later appear in Hemingway's book The Nick Adams Stories. The inclusion of existing people would be a feature of Hemingway's stories from then on. Sep Jingan draws on tales from traditional Indian knowledge. It is the name of a dog who saved Billy's life. Billy tells the story of an Indian named Paul Black Bird, who killed the game warden who caught him illegally spearfishing. The warden was Billy's cousin, so Billy sought revenge and tracked Paul with his faithful dog, Sepi Jingan. Two years later, on the Fourth of July, people found Paul Black Bird dead on the train tracks. They thought that he had gotten drunk and had himself killed by a train. But Billy knows better. On that very day, he and his dog had run into Paul. The problem was that Paul saw them first and knocked Billy to the ground with a pike-pole. While Paul toyed with his prey, Sepi Jingan crawled toward him from behind and attacked and killed Paul. Billy then put Paul on the tracks, causing people to conclude that Paul had lain down on the train tracks in a drunken stupor.

In these three stories, Hemingway established a style and pattern that is repeatedly found in his later work. All three have a surprise ending. In two of them, he portrayed Indians as protagonists. Even in his younger years, he sought places that influenced his writing most, and he never changed this pattern during his lifetime.

The experiences, surroundings, and happenings in Michigan find expression and can be recognized in much of Hemingway's work. On the contrary,

Hemingway's years spent in his primary home in Oak Park, Chicago, were hardly mentioned.

These influences are especially noticeable in *The Nick Adams Stories*. Here, Hemingway has shown a collection of short stories incorporating his alter ego, Nick Adams, published in various editions.

The book, as it is, was first published in 1972. In addition to previously published texts, it also contains work unpublished up to that time. The publisher chronologically sorted the stories written between 1922 and 1933 and divided them into five categories.

The first category, The Northern Forests, describes Michigan's landscape and living conditions. Hemingway's ability to define a landscape is evident from the beginning of the prologue:

'Of the place he had been a boy he had written well enough. As well as he could then.' That thought a dying writer in an early version of *The Snows of Kilimanjaro*. The writer, of course, was Hemingway. The place was Michigan of his boyhood summers, where he remembered himself as Nick Adams. As well as he could write then was very well indeed.

Seeking out places described in this book leads to the area surrounding Petoskey in the northwest section of Michigan's Lower Peninsula and to Seney in the

Upper Peninsula. The focal point is Horton Bay, a name that appears at the beginning of *The Nick Adams Stories*. Horton Bay and Horton Creek, the little river that flows around Horton Bay, are referred to in the fifth story, The Indians Moved Away.

This story takes place in Petoskey and its surroundings. Whereas Horton Bay is tiny, the focus is on Petoskey, the main town in Emmet County. It forms the most northerly point of the Lower Peninsula in Cheboygan County. The Hemingway family had their cottage on a site near Walloon Lake. 1905, they extended it to Longfield Farm on the other side of the lake. A local farmer cared for and worked the Hemingway land in their absence, as did the family during vacations. When Dr. Hemingway acquired the forty acres to provide them with food during summer vacation, he wished his children to learn and appreciate the value of honest physical work. 1917, he bought a further twenty acres and employed the farmer Warren Sumner.

With him, in this summer of 1917, Ernest spent most of the time. He was then eighteen, renovating the old farmhouse, cutting hay, and building an ice house. Sumner took ice blocks from the lake in winter and stored them to provide refrigeration for food and cold drinks for the Hemingway family in summer. Ernest fulfilled his father's wish for his son to learn the value of physical labor—at least for a while.

His father did not like Ernest spending much time reading books. He read all the classics, especially English authors, whose books were abundant in the family's library. An old nanny of Hemingway's recounted Dr. Hemingway's orders to take the books from Ernest with the words:

"Each evening, I'd search his cabin and take away all the books. When I'd tuck him in, he'd say good night, as sweet as could be. Then in the morning, I'd find books stuffed under the mattress, in the pillowcase, everywhere. He read all the time – and books way beyond his years."

Another person who occasionally helped at Windemere recalls:

"We saw a lot of Ernie when he was a kid, but later on, not so much. He went off in the woods, and he read a lot. He was sort of a loner. Always took this pup tent of his and went fishing somewhere alone."

For the Hemingway children, vacation times could be described as idyllic, even if Dr. Hemingway insisted on having them around him when felling trees or gathering fruits. There were duties and chores, such as going for milk to Grandpa Bacon's Farm, but these did not take anything away from the idyllic state, not even when, at the beginning of their stay, they had to help with repair work and improvements in the house and garden.

The journey from Oak Park to Michigan would have been strenuous at the time, but that would have been more than compensated for by the joyful anticipation of the time ahead.

To the northwest of Michigan, Hemingway's hometown of Chicago is on Lake Michigan's other side. The family journey to Windemere, loaded with cases and boxes, would begin at Chicago River Dock, usually on the steamer SS Manitou.

When the ship arrived in Harbor Springs in Michigan, they had to unload their luggage and bring it to the local station from which they traveled eleven miles away with the Grand Rapids & Indiana Railway that connected Harbor Springs and Petoskey. In this city, Petoskey, Hemingway set his first novel, *The Torrents of Spring.*

After completing the journey to Petoskey via the dune landscape surrounding the bay, they would change to Bourbon Station, only one block away from where they took a train directly to Walloon Lake Village, where they could finally get to Windemere by boat.

Grand Rapids & Indiana Station is still intact and being renovated. Today, it is used as a business and shopping center. On the other hand, Bourbon Station is now a parking lot.

When the journey was over, Ernest and his family immersed themselves in a natural world they knew and understood, which differed from the pressures of the so-called civilized world they had come from. However, it did not mean the children could ignore hygiene or appear unwashed and untidy at Windemere's table. But the countryside and the natural world where they spent those wonderful summers allowed them access to nature in its purest form.

The area is old Indian territory. The Ojibwe, Odawa, and Potawatomi Indians of Michigan, collectively known as the Anishinabek, also lived in Canada, Wisconsin, and Minnesota, north and south of Lake Huron and Lake Michigan. They lived from fishing, hunting, and harvesting wild water rice. Their lands were unsuitable for agriculture and were, thus, scorned by the white settlers. The Anishinabek, with their extended families and bands (sub-tribes), live nowadays on various reservations.

In the first story in his Nick Adams book, Hemingway relates his childhood experiences in which he Indians portrayed as active participants. For example, in the tale Indian Camp, Nick's father, the doctor, is called to assist with the birth of one child, and two Indians collect him in a rowing boat. Nick is allowed to travel with them. This short story contains brutality, misery, being in labor, and death—even hidden racism.

The story was first published in Paris in 1924 in a slim thirty-two-page book *in our time*. The lowercase was deliberate. Indian Camp was the first publication of a Nick Adams story. There is a dramatic moment in the book when Nick's father performs a cesarean section, without anesthesia, on the Indian woman with a sick husband lying in the upper bunk above her. Nick held a bowl while three women and a man held the woman down. After the birth, the husband was found with his throat cut—he had committed suicide during the delivery. To answer Nick's question about why, his father replied: "I don't know, Nick. He couldn't stand things, I guess."

But what was it indeed that he could not endure? Was it the screams of his wife or the "white" doctor's disregard?

When Nick asks his father to try and stop the woman from screaming, his response is cold and direct:

I don't have an anesthetic with me, and I don't hear them because they are not important.

After this statement, Hemingway wrote:

The husband in the upper bunk rolled over against the wall.

That Indian Camp, as the story is named, is most certainly the Indian settlement behind Windemere. All of the Indians who lived there worked as bark-peelers for the big tree-felling companies. When the mills closed, the base camp closed with it. Nick went to the Indian Camp with his father and uncle George.

Ernest's uncle, also named George, who lived nearby in Boyne City, claimed there was no truth in it after reading this story.

However, it proves nothing because it is unclear whether the uncle was around at the time of the incident. It is a fact, though, that Dr. Hemingway often helped out when the locals needed him, like assisting at births. In the story, the father-son relationship Ernest handled it delicately. When Nick's father discovered the dead husband, he regretted having brought his son with him. He apologized to him, but it was too late—Nick had seen everything. In this story, the apparent low esteem in which the white Americans hold the Indians is not immediately comprehensible. How the pregnant Indian woman's screams were ignored could be ascribed to the "doctor professionally conducting himself."

However, seeing Indians as a kind of "second class" did exist, and Hemingway described it graphically in another story, the Ten Indians. In it, after the Fourth of July festivities, Nick traveled home with a friend's parents. All along the way, their driver, Joe Garner, had to stop and drag Indians lying on the road to put them aside:

"That's nine of them," Joe said, "just between here and the edge of the town."
"Them Indians," said Mrs. Garner.

The Hemingway holiday home and Walloon Lake were somewhat west of and a few miles distant from Horton Bay. The lumber camp, close by, was known locally as the Indian Camp because most of the inhabitants were Indians who had provided the two stories mentioned above. Reading the Indian Camp story, I see that the father and son get on well enough. Although the father regretted having taken his young son with him when the Indian committed suicide at birth, it would appear his son's wish to be allowed to participate in his father's life actively.

Indeed, Ernest had always praised his father for having shown him everything he could and taught him things a father should teach his son.

Conversely, Ernest and his mother did not have a good relationship. Even when he was an eighteen-year-old reporter with The Kansas City Star, she made him justify, in a letter, his reasons for not going to Sunday church. He wrote to her then that he had to work till one after midnight and sometimes even later on Saturdays.

Sunday was the only day he could catch up on his sleep, and she should not worry about him not being a good Christian. His words: I am just as much as ever and pray every night and believe just as hard so cheer up! Just because I'm a cheerful Christian ought not to bother you.

But in the same letter, he made it clear that he could speak his mind: "Now mother I got awfully angry when I read what you wrote about Carl (Edgar) and Bill (Smith). I wanted to write immediately and say every-thing I thot (thought). But I waited, and I got all cooled off. But never having met Carl and knowing Bill only superficially you were mighty unjust. Carl … is the most sincere and real Christian I have ever known and he has had a better influence on me than any one I have ever known … I have never asked Bill what church he goes to because that doesn't matter. We both believe in God and Jesus Christ and have hopes for a hereafter and creeds don't matter."

Bill—William Smith Jr.—the person in question, was a good friend from their vacation times in Michi-gan.

He and his sister Kate (Katherine) spent the summer with their aunt. Kate would later become the wife of the American author John Dos Passos, who wrote, among other things, *Manhattan Transfer*. I meet her with Carl Edgar (also mentioned in the letter) in Hemingway's short story, Summer People. So, Ernest got to know Carl, whom he had named Odgar, through Bill and

Kate. He later shared a house with him in Kansas City. Odgar was in love with Kate. However, in Summer People, it is Hemingway's alter ego, Nick, who has a sexual relationship with her:

> Down the roads through the trees, he could see the white of the Bean house on its piles over the water. He did not want to go down to the dock. Everybody was down there swimming. He did not want Kate with Odgar around.
> He could see the car on the road beside the warehouse. Odgar and Kate were down there. Odgar, with that fried-fish look in his eye every time he looked at Kate. Didn't Odgar know anything? Kate would not ever marry him.

Yet later, Nick met Kate and Odgar, and on the way home, he arranged with Kate a late-night rendezvous:

> The car, in low gear, moved steadily up through the orchard. Kate put up her lips to Nick's ear. "In about an hour, Wemedge," she said. Nick pressed his thigh hard against hers. The car circled at the top of the hill above the orchard and stopped in front of the house. "Aunty is asleep. We've got to be quiet," Kate said.

They say their goodbyes, but later, Nick and Kate meet in the forest and make love. It does not, however, correspond with the real story. There is no evidence that Butstein, as Hemingway called Kate in life and the text, had a sexual relationship with Wemedge (Nick).

A letter from September 13, 1920, to Grace Quinlan, a girl from Petoskey Ernest had befriended, talks of a night when they were a bit drunk, during which Kate and Ernest entered a Catholic church and lit a candle. It would appear that this was the first time that Hemingway, raised as a strict Protestant, had entered a Catholic church.

This incident is worth mentioning because, later, Hemingway converted to Catholicism out of love for his second wife. On his visit to the church, he wrote:

> Then Kate and I went to the catholic church, and I prayed for all the things I want and won't ever got and we came out in a very fine mood and very shortly after to reward me the Lord sent me adventure with a touch of romance.

Having read this, one would not know what to think. In the same letter in which Hemingway mentions a romantic experience, he writes that he, on the way home, composed a poem for Grace, the letter's receiver. He considered Grace, six years his junior, as his sister.

It seems this is a smokescreen to cover up his true feelings for her—his interest and care are much more than I would expect from a brother-and-sister relationship.

In a letter dated August 21, 1921, he invites her and also Marjorie Bump (Marge), another girl from Petoskey, to his forthcoming wedding. He cautiously suggests it could all have been very different: "Know how you feel about my being too young to be married. Felt exactly the same."

He no longer had these feelings, and this was because of his bride, Hadley. Grace had been too young for marriage, even five years younger than the other girl, Marjorie. But what, given the compliments in his letters, if Grace had not been so young?

Kate, with whom he has "experienced a touch of romance," died tragically in a car accident in 1947 when her husband, John Dos Passos, blinded by the sun, collided with a truck that had come halfway across the road. Kate was tossed through the windscreen and died instantly. Dos Passos lost his right eye but survived.

Chapter 3

In his younger years, Windemere was where he had spent important and impressionable times during his summer vacations. Still, as he grew older, he began to spend more time in the company of Kate and her brother in Horton Bay, a small place nearby that attracted visitors in the summertime. Away from the family, Ernest was free to behave like a typical teenager, trying to impress girls, hanging out with friends, or using his gift for storytelling to fabricate tales of hunting and fishing or affairs in the far-off city of Chicago.

Horton Bay, named after a man called Horton, is no longer, with one exception, to be found on signposts. Nowadays, part of Bay, the name stands for Bay

Township, which is easy to find, leaving the road from Charlevoix and crossing a small bridge over Horton Creek. That little river appeared in Hemingway's work for the first time, in the story, The Indians Move Away.

The creek meanders around the place, a magical, picture-book landscape of little rapids weaving around mounds of sand, mossy stones, and the decaying tree remains, leaving a vital and vibrant impression in its path. Overgrown meadows and dense woodland present the pictures known from Hemingway's tales. As an observer, his depiction of the north of Michigan's natural beauty is just as sound today as in Hemingway's stories.

The Horton Creek is preserved as in the short stories mentioned and, I think, remains a template for other streams in other Hemingway stories. A photograph depicted little Ernest seen him fishing for trout with a far too big basket around his shoulders. He was seven years old. For me, this little river also symbolizes his childhood experiences of fishing, especially trout fishing, which he loved but was not always allowed to do. He did it anyway. In two passages in the story, The Last Good Country, his alter ego Nick fished for trout verbatim without permission. His sister asked him about it:

"Did you get many, Nickie?"
"I got twenty-six."

"Are they good ones?"

"Just the size they want for the dinners."

"Oh, Nickie, I wish you wouldn't sell them."

"She gives me a Dollar a pound." Nick Adams said …

"I'll go through the woods down to the inn beyond the point and sell her the trout," he told his sister. "She ordered them for dinners tonight. Right now, they want more trout dinners than chicken dinners. I don't know why. The trout are in good shape. I gutted them and they are wrapped in cheesecloth and they'll be cool and fresh …"

There are now several nature reserves around the bay. One of them is named after Nick Adams.

After crossing the bridge over Horton Bay Creek, the place comes into view with its few houses. In the story Up in Michigan, Hemingway describes it (sometimes spells it differently):

Hortons Bay, the town, was only five houses on the main road between Boyne City and Charlevoix. There was a general store and post office with a high false front and maybe a wagon hitched out in front, Smith's house, Stroud's house, Dillworth's house, Horton's house and

Van Hoosen's house. The houses were in a big grove of elm trees and the road was very sandy. There was farming country and timber each way up the road. Up the road a way was the Methodist church and down the road the other direction was the township school. The blacksmith shop was painted red and faced the school.

Upon arrival in the village, I was immediately drawn to the Horton Bay General Store, constructed in 1876. As it always was, it is the center of the township. Hemingway describes it not only in his short story Up in Michigan; it also seems to be the shape of Mr. Packard's Store in The Last Good Country. The shop contains pictures and memorabilia from and to Hemingway. And even more so in the next house, the Red Fox Inn, which Hemingway sometimes called Horton's house. On the front, it has Hemingway signs and a display case with memorabilia, pictures, clothing, accessories, books, and baseball caps with inscriptions: "Horton Bay" and "Hemingway." There is also a collection of other signs with different hints. One stated that the Red Fox Inn was built as a boarding house for loggers in 1878 and a hotel by James Wixham Fox in 1910 that his son, Vollie, took over in 1919. That year, they restored the house, which became an excellent venue for summer guests.

Most of the plaques and signs refer indeed to Hemingway. He had given the hotel a present of a helmet from the First World War, complete with a bullet hole. Or a sign suggests the building was referred to in the *Three Stories and Ten Poems*, published in Paris in 1923, and in the story Up in Michigan. Also, a plaque proudly states: "Hemingway slept here." It is correct, and he probably slept there more than once. There is confirmation about it before his first marriage, which he celebrated in the village.

Stepping into the former Inn, I was greeted by a sight that could only be described as a shrine to Hemingway. The room was filled with shelves laden with card racks, cabinets, chairs, and books. A wooden table in the center of the room held more books, pamphlets, and pictures. On the former reception desk were souvenirs, each one bearing the name Hemingway. The Red Fox Inn is a testament to the deep connection between Hemingway and this location.

I heard voices on the floor above me and shouted "Hello" a couple of times but did not get any answer. The conversation upstairs continued unabated. I could only make out a male voice, who seemed to carry on the conversation alone. After what felt like an hour, the person to the voice finally appeared, and I met James Vol Hartwell, Vollie and Lizza Fox's grandson, who was running the place and too pleased to reveal his family and the hotel's connection to the famous writer. Perhaps what he said was not entirely true, but that is unimportant. According to James, his grandfather had taught Hemingway fishing, but this cannot be true since, in the story, Fathers and Sons, Hemingway had expressly praised the father of his alter ego, Nick, for teaching him how to fish. True is, however, that Vollie was fishing with Ernest.

After visiting the Red Fox Inn, I went down to the bay on the opposite side of the road. I realized that much is, naturally, not in the condition it was when Hemingway described it. Nevertheless, the two houses at Dilworth Resort are still intact on Lake Street's left-hand side. Here, Hemingway had the "Wedding Breakfast" of his first marriage, as mentioned in the stories Summer People and Up in Michigan.

Both houses are still in possession of the Dilworth family, albeit the ex-husband of a granddaughter. The first of the two places, Pinehurst, is the original residence of the Dilworths, which was constructed in 1910 together with a forge since James Dilworth was a blacksmith. He later built the boarding house next door, which is still in business. Hemingway called it Shangri-La. However, the sign above its entrance door says Shangra La (this is not wrong, as I first thought, but it corresponds to Pakistani and not Indian spelling). The forge is no longer in its original state but as a replica.

Apart from roads that are no longer the sand paths in the stories, you can still get a clear impression of the place described by Hemingway. At the end of Lake Street, there used to be a dock that I learned from *The Nick Adams Stories*. Still intact, on the other side of the bay, is the old boathouse, seen as the background to a photo of the young Hemingway taken in 1919 after he had returned from The First World War, wounded and decorated as a hero—and also proudly displaying three freshly caught trout in his hand. I have used this photo for the cover design of this book.

The boathouse on the place where Horton Creek flows into the bay is referred to in the story The End of Something. I could be taken on in my mind and experience the course of a boat trip described by Hemingway in this story. It begins with a flashback to the closure of the great mill, which had been, to a great extent, the primary source of income for the people of Horton Bay:

In the old days, Horton Bay was a lumbering town. No one who lived in it was out of the sound of the big saws in the mill by the lake. Then one year there were no more logs to make lumber. The lumber schooners came into the bay and were loaded with the cut of the mill that stood stacked in the yard. All the piles of lumber were carried away. The big mill building had all its machinery that was removable taken out and hoisted on board one of the schooners by the man who had worked in the mill. The schooner moved out of the bay toward the open lake, carrying the two great saws, the traveling carriage that hurled the logs against the revolving, circular saws, and all the rollers, wheels, belts, and iron piled on a hull-deep load of lumber. Its open hold covered with canvas and lashed tight, the sails of the schooner filled and it moved out into the open lake, carrying with it anything that had made the mill a mill and Horton Bay a town.

The story begins with Nick and Marjorie rowing by the old disused mill. It is the year of that trout photo, where I see Hemingway as a handsome, bright, and happy young man. Despite his traumatic war experiences, he appears interested, dynamic, and strong—a direct contrast and light-years away from the pictures of the sick, overweight, depressive, and untidy Hemingway of later years. It makes me sad when comparing them.

However, he is not as bright and breezy on the boat trip as he appears in that picture of him. He and Marjorie have been fishing and, afterward, land for a picnic near the boathouse. Nick is in a bad mood, and when Marjorie asks him what happened to him, he tells her the truth: "It isn't fun anymore. Not any of it."

His remarks are rude and unambiguous; Nick has been Marjorie rudely rejected. Later, after she returns by boat alone and is disappointed, Nick's friend Bill comes out of the forest. He wonders if the girl luckily went away. Nick confirms she is. Bill then asks if there has been a scene. No, not, according to Nick. When Bill wants to know his feelings, Nick asks him to let him alone.

The story is somewhat autobiographical. That Bill is Bill Smith, with whom Hemingway spent the summer in Michigan. Marjorie did exist, but the episode is far from reality.

On the contrary, when Marjorie learned that Hemingway had used her name without her permission, she was agitated. Shortly before she died in 1987, she retold her daughter, Georgie, the whole story. From Georgie's book, we learn that Marjorie had always felt deeply hurt by Hemingway's portrayal of her in literature, which had nothing to do with authenticity: "I felt humiliated to be the object of their pity when they read about me as the young lady to whom Nick (as Ernest) had spoken these words about our relationship: 'It isn't fun anymore.'"

Later, she avoided telling her surroundings that she had known Hemingway. She was haunted by it and went so far as to have her middle name, Lucy, and not Marjorie, on her gravestone; at least she could finally be consoled. Ernest once wrote to say "sorry."

His exact words: "Everything understood is everything forgiven."

Carlos Baker, Hemingway's authorized biographer, describes the first meeting of Hemingway and Marjorie in the summer of 1919 when he was twenty:

She was seventeen, with red hair and freckles, dimpled cheeks, and a sunny disposition. Marjorie and her friend Connie Curtis had come from Petoskey to wait on tables at Mrs. Dilworth's.

But this is not true—even if this version of the story is not only found with Carlos Baker but almost always when speculating about Marjorie and Ernest in Horton Bay.

Repetition, as it proves, is indeed no guarantee of veracity. Tales get passed on, and people pass them on believing what they want to think.

Marjorie was born in Petoskey on August 24, 1901. According to her, she did not come to Horton Bay to work as a waitress; Ernest and Marjorie first met in 1915 and not in 1919. Her account: "The first time I saw Ernest Hemingway, I was walking back from Horton's Creek, where I had caught my first fish with a cane pole. Both of my hands were full of fish, and I was so proud and excited that I forgot to be afraid to talk to an older boy even though I didn't even know his name. I wasn't yet fourteen as my birthday would be coming up on August 24.

During the first meeting, Ernest probably saw me as a short, young teenager with red hair, green eyes, and freckles. What I saw was a tall, handsome boy with dark eyes who appeared to be about sixteen. Ernest stopped to admire my fish."

She had come to Horton Bay to visit her uncle, Professor Ernest Ohle, who had a holiday home there. At the same time, Ernest had seen his friend Bill Smith. At the end of their first meeting, Hemingway made a move toward her: "Well, Red, I like your beautiful fish, and since you're such a sport, I might take you with me to troll for rainbow trouts some day at the point."

"Would you really, truly? You won't forget, will you?"

"No chance of that. I need an extra hand with the boat, and you'll do."

Marjorie added: "Happily for me, Ernest did not forget his offer. It extended throughout my adolescent years as he often found the time to take me fishing for rainbow trout, bass, and perch in Horton Bay."

After that, Marjorie and Ernest met regularly. Marjorie's cousin, William Ohle, describes a meal at his parent's house opposite Dilworths' residence, which took place in 1917: "Ernest … sat uncomfortably at the table, speaking in monosyllables as my mother tried to keep conversation going."

But Marjorie spent more time with Hemingway's sisters, especially Ursula, who was her age. Those who doubt the facts that Ernest and Marjorie met at an early age—since this regard came from Marjorie's side—need to look no further than the pen of Hemingway himself for their verification. On December 6, 1917, when he was already in the army, he wrote to his parents from Kansas City:

"I got another Army thing the other day too that is great. An Army slip on sweater. Khaki wool. Marge Bump knitted it for me, and it is a peach of a sweater."

How could Hemingway have worn a "peach of a sweater" that Marjorie Bump had knitted him in 1917 when, in Baker's words, Ernest first had met and had a summer romance with her in 1919?

This letter is awkwardly not included in Hemingway's letter collection, edited by Carlos Baker.

Ernest and Marjorie did have a relationship. Maybe a romance. The fishing and boat trip was intended as an opportunity to finish the affair of the characters from Nick and Marjorie.

This is obvious not only from Bill's questions but also from the following story, The Three Day Blow, in which Bill says, "It's a good thing" that Nick finished with Marge:

"It was the only thing to do. If you hadn't, by now, you'd be back home working, trying to get enough money to get married."…

Nick said nothing … All he knew was that he once had Marjorie and that he had lost her. She was gone, and he had sent her away. That was all that mattered. He might never see her again. Probably, he never would. It was all gone, finished …

"If you had gone on that way, we wouldn't be here now," Bill said.

That was true. His original plan had been to go down home and get a job. Then he had planned to stay in Charlevoix all winter so he could be near Marge: Now he did not know what he was going to do … He had talked to her about how they would go to Italy together and the fun they would have. Places they would be together. It was all gone now. Something got out of him.

From this excerpt and further discussion, it is clear that Nick and Marge were not engaged but had intended to marry.

Nick wanted to spend the winter in the city to be closer to Marge, but he did not particularly like Marge's mother and stepfather. Nick was confused and felt sorry for how he had treated Marge, as stated in the story:

"going into town on Saturday," where he wanted to meet her and improve things.

There is little doubt that Marjorie's mother did not like Ernest in reality, as Marjorie has mentioned, and there seem to be reasons for the mother not liking him. According to her, Hemmingway had seriously considered marrying Marjorie.

However, his intention has more to do with material things and less with romance. Marjorie's mother had said that Ernest once had discussed marriage with her. But she had replied that her daughter was too young and should wait until they graduated from college before considering an engagement or marriage. During this conversation, Ernest asked Marjorie's mother if it was true that her daughter would inherit money from her grandmother, which was confirmed. But the inheritance would only be received after the death of her grandmother. Ernest needed money for writing then and had probably thought Marjorie could help.

Marjorie, aka Marge in the *Nick Adams* stories, was just part of the Michigan idyll that Hemingway describes when writing about summers and other times spent there. Ernest and Marjorie's first meeting was incredibly idyllic: creeks, fishing, and an innocent girl meets an innocent boy on the road. This perfect world ended six years later when Hemingway married his first wife, Hadley, and turned his back on Michigan.

From his stories, it is clear there had been much more than friendship between Marjorie and Ernest in that perfect summer and autumn of 1919. It was not just the holiday romance that it is thought to have been.

The facts suggest that it was a relationship that had carried on for years, but I have not found details on the romantic aspects of their time together.

I can only speculate about the romance of 1919, but I can conclude that there had been a relationship from Ernest's conversation on the marriage with Marjorie's mother. I have not every answer, of course, but the biographer Kenneth S. Lynn has even fewer when he takes it one absurd step further: he contends that in the two stories, The End of Something and The Three Day Blow, Marge is the young embodiment of Hemingway's first wife, Hadley and not Marjorie from Petoskey at all.

Lynn's insights probably missed the point, as seen in a letter of Christmas Eve, 1925, which Hemingway wrote to F. Scott Fitzgerald (who was working then on his famous *Great Gatsby*). The letter shows Hadley was not intended: "The only story Hadley appears in is Out of Season."

The two stories involving Marjorie are from the time before this letter. Why did Kenneth S. Lynn ignore some important facts? For me, his style is to ignore the facts even when they speak against him. I also question

Lynn's accounts of Hemingway's war experiences and will come to it later.

On the other hand, it is not always possible in literature to ascertain what initiates a story or any driving force behind it. In Hemingway's texts, there might be actual incidents, landscapes, and places in Michigan that, only under other circumstances, would correspond with the facts. However, considering the facts is different from what it is about.

In retrospect, it is not about the authenticity of Hemmingway's descriptions but concerns his literary concept and his stories' subject matter.

A writer sees the world from his perspective. The readers are allowed access, but his and readers' worlds would not necessarily correspond. Everyone has and shapes their inner world. The feelings and emotions described by Hemingway are so intense that it would be difficult not to ascribe them to the young Ernest as actual happenings and instead be seen as figments of imagination in his stories. Gentleness and sensitivity were seen in quiet moments, and his need for affection is as much evidenced in Hemingway's literary work.

Whether Marjorie or Hadley appears in both stories as real is theoretical and unimportant for Hemingway's writing or opinion on states of mind. Marjorie's facts are indisputable; whether or not she is the character in the stories is open to dispute. However, in both stories, I read about young people going through their experience of a relationship, knowing that it could end in marriage. In this case, it does not. Young Hemingway's world was preserved in his writing, which allows me to see into his life and the landscape of Michigan a century later.

The landscape encountered by Hemingway and other people at the beginning of the twentieth century has, naturally, been adapted and altered by time. However, the changes have not been as dramatic as in other parts, given the almost one hundred years timeframe.

At least, in Horton Bay, I did not have the impression of a lost or another world. Hemingway and his Nick Adams stories are still recognizable. However, the earlier Michigan is nowhere to be seen. At the turn of the twentieth century, the countryside changed dramatically when the old forests were exhausted, and deforestation began to spread grave. Hemingway says he was sickened by the ruined American landscape and "terribly" upset by the loss of the native ancient forests and pristine rivers.

Chapter 4

I can reconstruct the state of the Northern Michigan landscape from earlier times, using Dr. Hemingway's diary sketches and photos from his automobile trip with his wife, Grace, and sons Ernest and Leicester in the summer of 1917. The whole family would typically have traveled from Chicago by boat and train. Still, this time, only their daughters traveled that way.

The journey took five days by car. They slept in tents and fished for food, and with the roads in such terrible condition, the trip was a real adventure. Detours added 100 miles to the scheduled 487. They had a shovel to get the car going again when they got stuck.

The last 31 miles from Traverse City to Walloon Lake were exceptionally precarious. The sand roads were so bad that they could only drive an average of about eight miles per hour. Another tool, an ax, came in handy to chop branches that had fallen across the road in places. It even became embarrassing when, under a farmer's watchful eye and ironic smile, their Model T Ford got stuck and had to be rescued by horses. On the way back, they (and the car) traveled by boat.

Things are very different nowadays. The shovel and ax need no longer be companions on an automobile trip to Northern Michigan. However, perhaps Hemingway might not have approved of this because, even then, he commented critically about the interference with nature in his writing. He wouldn't have even experienced the change to its full extent. Considering what Ernest would have faced then, it looks like he exaggerated. For example, in his complaints, he talks about water pollution and waste, which were true, a vast topic of discussion in Chicago at the turn of the twentieth century. The solution was, as he has described, a flood relief channel. However, Chicago is situated on the southwest coast of Lake Michigan and part of Illinois.

In contrast, the area around Petoskey, where Hemingway spent his vacation in "his Michigan," is northeast of the lake.

He could only have known about deforestation by hearsay. But are environmental problems not of great importance for a writer? His disappointment about the changes taking place in Michigan is genuine. In 1947, he wrote to his colleague, William Faulkner: "My own country gone. Trees cut down. Nothing left but gas stations, sub-divisions where we hunted snipe on the prairie, etc. ..."

His sadness at the violation of the landscape is clearly expressed in the story The End of Something when Nick and Marjorie are out rowing on Horton Bay. The story begins with lamenting the closure and disrepair of the great mill: "What makes a windmill a windmill and what makes a town a town."

The loss of the last ancient forests brought change and damage to the Michigan landscape. When the loggers had cut down the trees and then the train tracks neglected, the towns died, and houses, apart from a handful, fell into disrepair or were ruined altogether. However, the changes that have taken place from Hemingway's childhood and youth to the present day have not been too drastic.

Today, I drove the road described in the story, The Indians Moved Away, and I could see that it is still readily identifiable.

The road ran straight uphill from Grandpa Bacon's farm to Petoskey. Along the edge of the trees, it went up the steep and sandy hill to disappear in the woods, where the long slope of fields stopped short against the hardwood timber.

Grandpa Bacon was this Henry Bacon who had sold them the site for their cottage, Windemere, in 1898. The Bacons and Hemingways became good friends. Before the Hemingways bought their farm, Henry provided them with milk, meat, butter, and vegetables, and the Hemingway children became acquainted with life in a rural environment for the first time. In return, Dr. Hemingway provided the Bacons with medical care at little or no cost. Ernest gave Henry Bacon a tiny place in history by including his illustrative directions to Petoskey in one of his short stories.

Nowadays, the road is, naturally, not in the same condition as Hemingway described it about a hundred years ago. A car built to today's standards could hardly have mastered the journey without assistance in those days when the roads were unsealed and uphill meant conquering a sandy slope.

However, I traveled up and down hills, undisturbed, rejoicing in the beauty of the surroundings from the hilltops. As is often the case in the USA, I could travel miles and miles up and down on seemingly endless roads.

And although Hemingway might not have welcomed the changes to the landscape, he loved it just the same. From his remark to his first wife, Hadley, when they drove along Little Traverse Bay, I can figure out when Hemingway said: "See all that. Talk about the beauty of the Bay of Naples! I've seen them both, and no place is more beautiful than Little Traverse in its autumn colors."

By the way, I also have seen both and Little Traverse Bay in the fall as well and can confirm his opinion.

Hemingway describes a particular landscape in The Last Good Country—a woodland area northeast of Horton Bay. However, it is not only his description of the landscape that impresses me; his outline of the destruction wreaked upon the forests of Michigan by people and loggers is graphic. Nick and his sister discuss this while traveling together:

> They came from the hot sun of the slashing into the shade of the great trees. The slashing had run up to the top of a ridge, and then the forest began. They were walking on the brown forest floor now, and it was springy and cool under their feet. There was no underbrush, and the trunks of the trees rose sixty feet high before any branches. No sun came through as they walked. His sister walked close to him.
> "I'm not scared, Nickie. But it makes me feel very strange."

"Me too," Nick said. "Always."

"I never was in wood like these."

"This is all the virgin timber left around here ...
Don't worry. There it's cheerful. You just enjoy
this, Littless. This is good for you. This is the way
forests were left. Nobody gets in here ever."

The Last Good Country is not a short story but
the beginning of a novel that, sadly, Hemingway never
completed. In sixty-three pages, he managed to build up
so much tension that it almost hurts, considering that
the story comes to an end at the heart of it. The idea for
it refers to his youth in 1915, to an unusual incident involving Hemingway and a heron. Around his sixteenth
birthday (near July 21), Hemingway managed to startle
a heron and shoot it from the boat. He had wanted to
give it to his father as a present because there was no
heron in their collection of stuffed animals.

Ernest wrapped the heron in newspaper and hid
it in his boat. Unluckily, the son of the local game warden observed him, snitched it, and the warden started
questioning him. Hemingway pretended he had got the
heron from an unknown man. Nevertheless, two
strange men appeared at Windemere the next day to ask
the same questions. Ernest had told his mother the
whole story, and she suggested he should go and hide in
the Longfield farm on the other side of the lake.

As a result, Ernest is absent when the two men make their visit to the house. In a letter to her husband, dated July 30, 1915, Ernest's mother recounts the encounter with the men in this manner: "I thought them burglars or fiends of some sort. They had a beastly, insinuating, sneering way and would not state their business. They fired question after question … I said if you know so much about my business and that of my family, you don't need to give me any further impudence. This tackling a lone woman and her little children without giving you're your business or authority and asking impudent questions is not the way to behave yourselves, and just you remember it the next time."

After that visit, Grace Hemingway sent Ernest a message to find a better hiding place. He took her advice.

First, however, went to Jim Dilworth and his wife, Liz, who had a chicken grill business in Pinehurst Cottage. Still on the run from the gamekeepers, he found refuge in his uncle's summer house close to Ironton and on the opposite side of Lake Charlevoix. Later, on his father's advice, Ernest admitted his guilt to authorities and paid the fifteen dollars fine. Besides visiting his uncle, he included the incident in The Last Good Country draft.

One of Hemingway's sisters also plays a role in the unfinished novel. She accompanies him on the run.

The real story tells that, at the time of the shooting of the heron, his sister Sanny—about ten and a half years old then—was present at the moment. However, from Hemingway's written lines in *The Nick Adams Stories*, I am doubtful that the character whom he gave the pet name, Littless, had to do with his sister Sanny. Most probably, it was Ursula. In the story, he described her as follows:

> His sister was tanned brown, with dark brown eyes and dark brown hair with yellow streaks from the sun. he and Nick loved each other and did not love the others.

Ursula's hair and eyes were dark brown, and there is much to indicate that she was Nick's sister, Littless. The special relationship that Hemingway and his sisters share is further shown when, in the story Fathers and Sons, Nick comments on his father's unpleasant smell. Nick loved his father but hated the smell of him. Once, he had to wear a suit of his father's underwear that had gotten too small for him; it made Nick feel sick. He took it off and put it under two stones in the creek. His father whipped him for lying when he came home and said he had lost it. Afterward, he had sat inside the woodshed with the door open. His shotgun loaded and cocked, looking across at his father sitting on the screen porch reading the paper, and thought, 'I can blow him to hell. I can kill him.' Finally, he felt his anger go out of him, and he seemed a little sick about it, holding the gun that his father had given him.

The relationship between Nick and Littless in The Last Good Country exceeds what we usually understand as a brother-and-sister relationship. This impression filters through the whole story, which begins with Littless kissing her brother with both arms wrapped around him. Later Nick says to her: "I'd like to kiss you."

The unique attraction becomes more explicit in the scene where Littless sits on Nick's lap and snuggles her head against his cheek. They talk, and after some time, Nick tells her to get off his lap because he has to prepare a meal. She then asks if she can kiss him while he takes care of the meal.

Some commentators suggested he was sexually aroused and, therefore, asking his sister to get off his lap, which I found hard to imagine given the tone of the scene. However, it was clear from the text that Nick was aware of and concerned about this bond, which went beyond a typical brother-sister relationship:

> He loved his sister very much, and she loved him very much. But, he thought, I guess those things straighten out. At least, I hope so.

However, this is different from Littless's outlook on life. Her dreams about the future life are made clear at breakfast. Nick asks:

"Did you sleep all night?"
"I'm still asleep. Nickie, can we always stay here?
"I don't think so. You'd grow up and have to get married."
"I'm going to get married to you anyway. I want to be your common-law wife. I read about it in the paper."
"That's where you read about the Unwritten Law."
"Sure. I'm going to be your common-law wife under the Unwritten Law. Can't I, Nickie?"
"No."
"I will. I'll surprise you. All you have to do is to live a certain time as a man and wife. I'll get them to count this time now. It's just like homestead-ing."
"I won't let you file."
"You can't help yourself. That's the Unwritten Law. I've thought it out lots of times. I'll get the cards printed. Mrs. Nick Adams, Cross Village – common-law wife. I'll hand these out to a few people openly each year until the time's up."

"I don't think it would work."

"I've got another scheme. We'll have a couple of children while I'm a minor. Then you have to marry me under the Unwritten Law."

"That's not Unwritten Law."

"I get mixed upon it."

"Anyway, nobody knows yet if it works."

"It must," she said.

Here again, I can see how the impetus comes from the younger sister—an infatuation that, most probably, went beyond what's considered normal. As the passages referring to the story show, Nick's expectations, at the time and for the future, do not correspond with those of his younger sister.

Ernest Hemingway felt very close to his sister Ursula and always spoke fondly of her in real life. There is no evidence of an incestuous relationship between Ernest and her or any of his other sisters. Regarding his other sisters, he was more positively disposed to Sanny than his oldest sister, Marceline, which was remarkable because their mother considered Ernest and Marceline, more or less, twins, and raised them as such. It seems the mother had tried to unite them in a special brother-sister bond.

In a letter to his publisher, Charles Scribner, in 1949, Ernest wrote that his mother failed. This way, he clears up any misconceptions there might have been about him and his relationships with his sisters. He also complained about an article in that he appeared in the magazine McCall's: "How could this miserable McCall woman possess the gall to even think of writing about my family and me? How cheek of her to write about how I differ from my less talented brothers and sisters: my sister, Marceline, the witch; my lovely sister, Ura (a pet name for Ursula); and my younger sister, Sanny, who played like an angel's harp on the boys' team at school."

It would seem to be sure that his sister, Ursula, had used to be Nick's sister in The Last Good Country. Ernest stayed in close contact with her throughout his life, even later when she moved to Honolulu.

Ursula remained enthralled by her elder brother throughout her life, and he was vice versa. It might have had to do with her being fascinated by him, referred to in the short story, in the words where she suggests they get married when they grow up.

There is further proof of her love for her brother in her almost submissive behavior shortly after her brother returns, wounded from the war. Ursula was seventeen years old and would sleep on the step outside Ernest's bedroom door to be awake when he returned home. When he came, she would not part from him even for a moment because she felt it was unsuitable for a man to drink alone. She drank soft drinks with him until he fell asleep, then slept by him to ensure he would not be alone at night. They would sleep with the light on unless she switched it off after he had gone to sleep, but she would remain awake and switch the light on again if he awakened.

Hemingway himself wrote about it extensively and in detail. Between the lines is evidence Hemingway's war wounds were mental as well as physical. Perhaps Ursula was the only family member that he had confided in regarding the extent of his injuries, which would explain her belief in the need to care for him on those long nights.

Consequently, she was the one family member he had loved most. Ursula's caring for the wellbeing of her brother, returning wounded from the war, is remarkable. How appropriately it was is demonstrated in a poem Hemingway wrote in 1921, with the meaningful title: "Killed Piave-July 8-1918", the very day Hemingway was seriously wounded.

> Desire and
> All the sweet pulsing aches
> And gentle hurting
> What were you,
> Are gone into the sullen dark.
> Now in the night, you come unsmiling

To lie with me
A dull, cold, rigid bayonet
On my hot-swollen, throbbing soul.
Cover my eyes with your pinions
Dark bird of night …
Dip with your beak to my lips
But cover my eyes with your pinions.

It is worth mentioning that Ursula set up the Ernest Hemingway Memorial Award for Creative Writing after his death at the University of Hawaii. She took her own life five years later when she found out that she had incurable cancer.

The Hemingway family established an unspeakably tragic "tradition" in which four of the eight family members and one of Hemingway's granddaughters committed suicide.

At forty-two, Margaux Hemingway, a pretty famous actress, took her life on the anniversary of her grandfather's death in 1996. Male family members: the father, Dr. Clarence Hemingway, and the sons, Ernest and Leicester, took their lives in the same manner: they shot themselves.

The suicides of Ernest and Ursula become all the more tragic when one considers the brother-sister relationship, Nick and Littless—as Hemingway they called in the story.

Despite ups and downs, they seem to wander through the natural world relatively carefreely. There appears to be a future for them, albeit uncertain and seemingly impossible at times, but part of their scheme of dreams— dreams that yearn for a bright and carefree future. These are two children living in harmony with nature who see life as valuable and worth living. Two scenes in the story, The Last Good Country, throw light on their mutual attraction and Ursula's sensitive nature. In the first, I became aware of the nostalgic sadness that escaping from Horton Bay causes the brother and sister:

> When they reached the top of the hill, they looked back and saw the lake in the moonlight. It was clear enough to see the dark point, and beyond were the hills of the far shore.
> "We might as well say goodbye to it," Nick Adams said.
> "Goodbye, Lake," Littless said. "I love you, too."

The second scene has to do with hunting. It shows that the passion for hunting is not just a question of upbringing and environment. It has more to do with character traits: Littless enjoyed the same upbringing and grew up in the same place yet has reservations about hunting, which could, of course, also have to do with her having a feminine nature:

They had gone on, and suddenly, Nick had raised the rifle and shot before his sister could see what he was looking at. Then, they heard the sound of an ample bird tossing and beating its wings to the ground. She saw Nick pumping the gun and shooting twice more … Nick went forward into the willows and picked up the three grouse and batted their heads against the butt of the rifle stock, and laid them out on the moss. His sister felt them, warm and full-breasted and beautiful feathered.

"Wait till we eat them," Nick said. He was very happy.

"I'm sorry for them now," his sister said. "They were enjoying the morning just like we were."

Chapter 5

The sister seems lovable, but how about the character Nick, and what about Hemingway himself?

As an author, he is an extraordinary personality, a writer of world renown whose work has survived far beyond his death and, I believe, will continue to shine. However, in real life, I cannot describe Hemingway as unique, rather the opposite. He behaved like one who was not committed to values of any kind.

The young author's sensitivity becomes clear to me when, in the story The Last Good Country, his little sister says, "I love you, too," as she leaves the lake. And when she empathetic shows compassion for all living beings (as for the dead birds) and takes joy in wandering with her brother through the almost pristine nature.

When I then look at the harmful circumstances of Hemingway's childhood and youth, I sense the tragedy in the offing—the life as an alcoholic and the depression.

Hemingway had a particular love of nature, which was a refuge for him, especially in his youth, and gave him the necessary impetus for his writing career later on. The unhappy life in his family and the post-traumatic stress disorder due to his war experiences favored the unstable parts of his character. They led to his subsequently insensitive behavior, for which I feel deep compassion. However, it would be wrong to accuse him of having a botched life because everything that led to his depressive behavior also determined his literary success.

Even Hemingway's first stories are characterized by his strong connection with nature and his talent for creating finely drawn, lifelike characters with few words. Only a writer like this can access the depths of the soul. An approach that remained closed to him in everyday life. This sensitive aspect was missing; or rather, he denied it out of fear that he would not be perceived as the strong man he thought he was. When one thinks of a childhood trying to compensate for a "weak father" and overcome a "domineering mother," how could he possibly have known anything better? Ernest's relationship with his mother described Major General Charles T. Lanham, who had been with him on several fronts of The Second World War: "He always referred to his mother as 'that bitch.' He must have told me a thousand times how much he hated her and in how many ways."

From Hemingway's description of the relationship, the real reasons are unclear. It seems inevitable that one of them would have been how she treated his father.

In his late thirties, Ernest wrote that he (the father) was married to a woman with whom he had no more in common "than a coyote has with a female poodle."

Later, Ernest made her responsible for his father's suicide, but the actual reason for it could have had to do with the state of his father's health. He had diabetes, among other diseases. There were money issues as well. An unfortunate investment in Florida led to financial difficulties. According to the story told by Ernest's brother, Leicester, their father had asked Ernest for money, to which he agreed immediately.

The letter, containing his intention to send the money, was delivered on December 6, 1928, the day Dr. Hemingway shot himself. His son's letter lay unopened in his room.

Although Ernest did not detail why he disliked his mother, I can draw conclusions based on how she behaved toward him. This behavior must have left scars on the son's soul.

She had wanted him to be more feminine, more a twin "sister" for his sister Marceline, who was a year his senior. His mother used to dress him in girl's clothes and treated him like a girl.

From when they began to walk, boys and girls could be distinguished by clothing and hairstyles, but not Ernest. His mother, Grace, was determined to treat Ernest and his sister Marceline as twins. It only ended when Ernest began attending kindergarten. Ernest and his sister wore the same clothes and slept in twin beds in the same room. They had the same toy dolls and were encouraged by their mother to do everything together. Later, she would send them on fishing trips, walking tours, or even visit friends together. She did everything she could to ensure Ernest and Marceline could be together. She had them go out together as a twosome or made them a present of a season ticket for the opera. Even after Ernest had begun to go out with girls, she saw they went to a student ball as a couple. Her delusion reached a notable high point when she kept Marceline back a year to start school together.

Ernest, however, did not feel drawn to his sister. At twenty-two, his mother was concerned about the chill between him and his sister. And she suggested Marceline was shattered, distraught, and a bundle of nerves since she had heard of his upcoming wedding. She requested that he write about it to Marceline. But Ernest had no intention of it. He was not particularly interested in his sister's troubled soul, and his feelings for her were anything but loving or brotherly. In a letter to his other sister, Sanny, in August 1949, he wrote: "Marce, I always thought, from when I first knew her, which goes back now half a hundred years, of as a bitch complete with handles, want nothing to do with her ever."

It is undoubtedly true that Marceline felt her brother did not care for her. Her impression is probably why she did not attend Ernest's wedding, something that would not have bothered the groom in particular.

Anyone interested in the family or who knew them in any way knows Ernest's mother's manipulative influence over her son. In biographies, one can read that he willingly followed her and played Marceline's "sister" role, although he also insisted on being a boy.

The choice of clothes during their holiday in Michigan shows that the mother was also not always consistent in her wish that Ernest behaves like a girl.

From early childhood, having an identical sister was a deep-seated disturbance in Hemingway's definition of himself. His sexual identity and physical awareness culminated in the question: "Am I a boy or a girl?" or "What am I, or what am I not?"

When a boy is confused about his ego, body, and sexual identity, it has far-reaching consequences for his later development. In particular, for his relationship with the opposite sex.

The ill feeling between Ernest and his mother appears to have reached its highest point after returning from the war in Europe.

There was constant tension between them—mostly criticism of his rejection of her wishes that he should have gone to college. His mother was in bad physical condition, plagued with headaches and gout in her shoulders and arms. In this atmosphere, Ernest spent his time at home trying to write short stories, all rejected by publishers. When he was not writing, he enjoyed his time with friends.

During the early summer of 1919, the Hemingway family, as was their tradition, journeyed to Michigan. The tension between mother and son was palpable, with Ernest feeling increasingly like a misunderstood child. In his mother's eyes, he was a stubborn boy who failed to contribute at home, idly smoking and reading, speeding around town with his friend Bill in his car, or dating a high school girl named Marjorie.

This perception deeply upset Ernest, who, despite his life experiences, felt he was still treated like a little boy by his mother. Ernest's mother was a woman of peculiarities, particularly when it came to her understanding of motherly love. Her mindset can be gleaned from a letter she wrote a year later, when she, after an argument, expelled her twenty-one-year-old son from their Windemere home.

She must have spent considerable time thinking about what she would say to him and carefully thought it out. In that letter, she compares a mother's love to a bank account—a support fund drawn upon for the first five years. During this time, the mother is a kind of biologically enslaved person. Afterward, the account continues to be drawn upon, albeit in smaller quantities. Later, some smaller deposits are expected: Favors, considerations, and gratitude. After puberty, the account is noticeably empty yet continues to be paid out through love and understanding. But now, according to Ernest's mother, it is time to start to pay back in sizable sums. There is a general payback list, which sometimes becomes detailed and demanding. Examples would be taking home flowers, fruit, snacks, or something pretty to wear or greeting the mother with a kiss or an embrace. Perhaps bills could be quietly paid to take some pressure off the mother.

Grace knows mothers who get that and much more from their sons. She does not get any of it from her son, though. Reproaches follow the account overdraft comparison. She refers to his ancestry: "You come from a line of gentlemen." In the end, she expresses the hope that he will come to his senses, and should this happen, salvation in the form of love could await him.

It's hard to believe, but the letter does exist. I conclude that Ernest's mother was a sad woman deeply disappointed in her life.

As a young girl, Grace was a talented singer who could concentrate on her music lessons with her parents' full support. She felt she had enough talent to have an opera singer career and prepared for a life on stage. When she graduated from High School, she taught music and, at the same time, kept up her voice training.

However, her hopes of a great career did not materialize. In 1896, she debuted in Madison Square Garden, New York, where she suffered such severe headaches that she gave up rather than not succeed.

Against the better judgment of her singing teacher, she ended her career and married Dr. Clarence Hemingway. Her parents raised her to stay out of the kitchen. But now, she suddenly had to manage the life of a housewife.

The dreams of a great career were over, and these expectations were unfulfilled and frustrated. A woman who has reached such a high grade or position in life will often try to live out her own failed ambitions in their children. The husband, not understanding or knowing these unfulfilled needs, is usually more in the way than anything else.

Instead of providing the children love and care, they become objects of a particular study. She governs the necessary care and attention by how they are expected to behave.

Hemingway's relationship with his mother was problematic or very bad. It does not change in his adult life, even after her death. He stayed away from his mother's funeral.

The situation was different with his father. Ernest declined him as well because he saw him as a coward. However, the weakness in his father that he rejected was attributed to his mother. If there is no deep emotional bond with the mother, it can be difficult for the child and the father. A more intense reading of the Nick Adams story Fathers and Sons reveals how much Ernest must have loved his father.

The story was published in the short story collection *Winner Take Nothing* in 1933, five years after his father's death.

It is about a grandfather, father, and son and their relationship. When Nick Adams drives about the countryside with his young son, he remembers his own father, who had introduced him to fishing and hunting. He remembers his father's helplessness when explaining the things of life to him, but above all, he recognizes him as a great hunter.

When Hemingway created the character of Nick's father, I assume that the events and happenings in his young life could superimposed on the life of the young Hemingway. In this story, though, he writes with affection about his father:

> He was sentimental, and, like most sentimental people, he was both cruel and abused … All sentimental people are betrayed so many times … Nick was a boy. He was very grateful to him for two things: fishing and shooting. His father was a sound on those two things as he was unsound of sex, for instance, and Nick was glad that it had been that way; for someone has to give you your first gun or the opportunity to get it and use it, and you have to live where there is game or fish if you are to learn about them. Now, at thirty-eight, he loved to fish and to shoot precisely as much as when he first went with his father.

Despite being deprived and his emotional needs not being met by his father's strictness, it is understandable that the young Ernest, until he was sixteen, grew up only with sisters and desperately held on to his father's love. There would have been opportunities for his father to be there for him. To pass on his knowledge and experience to him as something special. In these special moments, there is the manly side of his father, the part usually hidden behind a domineering wife, moments when the father fulfilled deep longings in his son. On the death of Hemingway's father, F. Scott Fitzgerald wrote to him, and Ernest replied in a letter from December 9, 1928: "I was fond as hell of my father and feel too punk—also sick, etc.—to write a letter but wanted to thank you."

When his father could show his fatherly feelings, Ernest loved, liked, and honored him. But the mother was always in between the two of them. It was a terrible setup where a son felt drawn to a father who, in turn, was put down and humiliated by a mother who saw her son as "an investment."

Did Ernest have a chance of a better childhood? An opportunity not to become a victim of dependency and depression in his later life?

How could a growing boy or youth come to terms with all this? On the one hand, he has a father who means everything to him, but a father who is subservient to his wife on the other. The youth called this a "betrayal" and considered his father a "coward." His father's suicide in 1928 supports this insight: to end one's own life means not accepting it and withdrawing from it. Ernest's father shot himself as in his elderly life did Ernest, who in doing so failed in his lifelong wish not to be like his father.

So, Hemingway's path to the Nobel Prize had a specific expense: the price for his fame and extraordinary writing talent. He saw this Prize as the result and outcome of an unhappy childhood and youth. When one adds that the conditions of that time were male domination, and the first experience of an adult man's life was war, it is understandable that the masculine side of Ernest's personality was over-emphasized. Hemingway was severely injured in The First World War and honored for his bravery. These experiences preoccupied him throughout his life and impacted his work.

He lived the life of a public hero, perhaps placing too much emphasis on the body at the expense of his soul. Even from early youth, alcohol had been the substance that had masked the division of body and soul in him, but, as in most cases, it only appears to "help" in the short term. The suffering that followed resulted in depression.

If the illness does not find its way out, the life of a man becomes a torment, and suicide offers an immediate "solution" to the suffering or an "escape."

To avoid appearing a failure, he had to punch above his weight in all areas and aspects of life, which involved a lot of pretense, playacting, and talking himself up—these character traits he possessed in abundance. All other qualities of his were left to their own devices. Outpouring masculinity was the attribute he played in public and the world. His "controlled" life was one that he seemed to believe he had fully mastered.

However, the world was not as Hemingway had imagined it to be, and his behavior was not only admired. Continuing to paint a picture of himself and others was a laborious and exacting task, and the effect he had wanted to achieve was not always possible. In some respects, people around him were compassionate and sympathetic to him in his victim role.

Still, it is an illusion that one can lead a life of always expecting to please others or trying to prove something to oneself.

Hemingway's preparation for the ending of his life on the morning of that summer's day in Ketchum, Idaho, was a confirmation of the worst possible fears for those closest to him. His wife, Mary, slept as he went out to the verandah—his hunting shotgun loaded with two cartridges in his hands. He pulled both triggers at once.

A short time previously, Mary had found him motionless with a gun in his hand and had taken it from him. He had already tried to jump out of a plane. Another time walked almost intentionally into a rotating propeller as the aircraft was about to take off. This day, however, he "succeeded."

For the world, Hemingway probably showed only his manly side, focused on brevity. The reason, perhaps, was that his insecurity about his sexual identity, caused by his mother's attempt to bring him up as his sister Marceline's twin, would have influenced his understanding of manhood. It might compounded by a "weak" father who could not be a manly example. Ernest had four sisters. His brother, Leicester, was sixteen years his junior, which meant that apart from his father, he was surrounded by female family members. He did not want to be seen as weak or feminine. He had to appear strong because he had to suppress what he had hated most in his father: cowardice.

But not only Hemingway's suicide shows that it had been difficult for him to avoid the inevitable. After his death, Norman Mailer attested to it in an essay written for The Esquire entitled "The Big Bite":

Hemingway was probably not the brave man who sought trouble, adventure, and danger for excitement. The truth about his odyssey is perhaps just that he has fought all his life against cowardice and a hidden secret to commit suicide and that his inner landscape was a nightmare. He might have spent his nights wrestling with the deities. It could even be that the final evaluation of his work concluded that his failure was tragic, but his work was heroic. I imagine that he carried fears around that would have suffocated any weaker man than him.

In the words of a professional, this opinion sums up the twilight years of the gifted writer Hemingway. His tragic end suggests that he found the discrepancy between the public life he led and his actual inner person intolerable. If his work reflects on something wholly, it is the meaninglessness of many aspects of life and the cruelty of death.

He had offered his services as an ambulance man behind the front line in The First World War. Later, in the Spanish Civil War, he took a bank loan to support his literary voice and activity for the freedom fighters' cause. He was a war correspondent in The Second World War. He went on countless big game hunting expeditions in Africa and survived two plane crashes.

As he said, an unhappy childhood is the very best preparation for the life of a good writer, but his later life might also have helped him to become a great writer.

Considering all this, it is easy to understand and evaluate the nature and style of Hemingway's life as a sacrifice for literature.

Chapter 6

Ernest Hemingway's formation and upbringing did not make him into the brave and sturdy youth he saw himself to be, but rather someone who was much more sensitive and anxious, as can be deduced from the story Three Shots:

He was always a little frightened of the woods at night. He opened the flap of the tent and undressed, and lay very quietly between the blankets in the dark. The fire was burnt down to a bed of coals outside. Nick lay still and tried to go to sleep. There was no noise anywhere. Nick felt he could only hear the fox bark or an owl or anything, and he would be all right. He was not afraid of anything definite as yet. But he was getting very afraid … Last night in the tent, he had the same fear. He never had it except at night. It was more a realization than a fear at first. But it was always on the edge of fear and became fear very quickly when it started. As soon as he began to be really frightened, he took the rifle and poked the muzzle out the front of the tent and shot three times … He lay down to wait for his father's return and was asleep before his father and uncle put out their jack light on the other side of the lake.

The literature on Hemingway is full of psychologically tinged assumptions and conclusions, and I have also added one at the beginning of this chapter.

But these are assumptions, just like the one that Hemingway is said to have had castration anxieties or fetishes, described in detail in the book *Hemingway's Fetishism: Psychoanalysis and the Mirror of Manhood*. He is also said to have preferred boyish women, including those with short haircuts.

Or racial fetishism, which should become particularly evident in the manuscript *The Garden of Eden*, which was only published after Hemingway's death. Reference was also made to *The Nick Adams Stories*, in which Nick is said to have had his first sexual experiences with an Indian girl. I think one can make a lot of assumptions, and there are certainly signs that Hemingway's macho behavior was not only in line with his desire for recognition but was also intended to cover up some parts of him that he did not like or that he did not know how to deal with. But the fact that he should surrounded himself with white women, even marrying four of them, to hide a racial fetish is too "far-fetched" for me.

Hemingway had grown up with sisters and was no stranger to the physical difference between boys and girls; these differences could not have remained unnoticed, especially with all their freedom and running around in summer months. Ernest's father taught him not only fishing and hunting but also swimming, and that at the same time as Marceline. As if it would have satisfied the mother's "twin wish," although unconsciously, since the father appeared to have been against the idea.

It was a special privilege for the Hemingway children in summer in Michigan to go swimming, naked, just before bedtime, a habit they kept up into their teenage years. Apart from the unverified incestuous relationship Ernest should have had with his sister Ursula, it would appear that the first girl he had seen in puberty was Prudence Boulton, previously mentioned in connection with Nick Adams' suspected racial fetishism, that Indian girl. She was the daughter of Nick Boulton, who, like all the Indians, worked at the sawmill. He appears in the story's first sentence, The Doctor and the Doctor's Wife. Hemingway referred to him as Dick, who came from the Indian camp to cut up logs for Nick's father and brought his son Eddy and another Indian, Bill Tabeshaw.

The story is interesting because, in the course of the story, the Indian accuses Nick's father of stealing timber, although he had explained that it had simply been a floating log that had fallen off a transport ship. He thought removing it from the water was better than letting it rot. The Indian insisted that Nick's father had stolen the timber, which resulted in a quarrel, and he sent the Indians away. The incident might have occurred because the argument between Nick's parents would indicate that Nick's mother (like Ernest's) was a practicing Christian who advised her husband to stay out of fights and arguments.

This story, published in 1924 in the journal Transatlantic, was praised by Ernest's father for the first time that he did about a text written by his son. It is confusing because Ernest portrayed him not in a positive light, neither in the fight with the Indians, where he is portrayed as a loudmouth, nor in conversation with his wife, where he meekly capitulates.

Ernest's father considered the story purely fictitious because, in real life, the Indian would have chopped up the old tree trunk, and the fight would not have taken place.

In a letter to his son, Dr. Hemingway praised him for his story and the fact that, as far as he could remember, Ernest would have been as young as twelve at the time of the incident. In the letter, he also writes that he would be delighted if Ernest could send him some of his work more often. This wish was incomprehensible in light of all that had happened earlier. Shortly before this, Dr. Hemingway had sent his son's book *in our time* back to the publisher.

The book in question was that little thirty-two-page book printed in Paris in 1924. In 1925, the following year, it was published in America with the same title. But this time, the style of the title had changed into capital letters, *In Our Time*. Ernest's parents ordered six copies of the first book.

After reading it, especially the lines where the character in the book, a war hero like Ernest, had infected gonorrhea from a salesgirl, they sent all of them back because, as Dr. Hemingway wrote, they did not wish to keep such "filth" in the house.

Anyway, Ernest was delighted by his father's praise of his story, The Doctor and the Doctor's Wife, and he wrote to him from Paris on March 20, 1925:

"I am so glad you liked the Doctor story. I put in Dick Boulton and Billy Tabeshaw as real people with their real names because it was pretty sure they would never read the Transatlantic Review. I've written a number of stories about the Michigan country—the country is always true—what happens in the stories is fiction."

As later letters show, this recognition by his father, which had delighted Hemingway at the beginning of his career, was an exception.

On February 5, 1927, in a letter to his mother addressed to both father and mother, he states that he finds it pitiful that he, as an author, has to justify himself to his parents. He wants to write books and not letters to them. If his books are not to their liking, perhaps that can change one day because: "You may never like anything I write, and then suddenly, you might like something very much."

Ernest was not ashamed of his work. Why should he have been? But he felt obliged to emphasize this in the letter: "… otherwise, I am in no way ashamed at all of the book."

His mother could not or would not accept what her son was doing. The public recognition his work was receiving changed nothing for her. That letter referred to the book *The Sun Also Rises*, which was a huge success. The quality of his writing does not justify a shame. He stated he would only be ashamed if he had not done his work correctly, if he had not entirely captured the people and their character, or if they had not come alive in the eye of the reader. Even if the book is unpleasant or uncomfortable, "it is not more unpleasant than the real lives of some of the leading families in Oak Park, Chicago," where the Hemingway family lived. Hemingway had to point out to his mother things that he, as a writer, took for granted and which were understood by the neutral reader of sound mind: Books dealt with the dark underbelly of life and questioned what is acceptable because, in public day-to-day life, people attempt to show themselves up only in their best light.

He tried to get his mother to see his point of view when addressing the artist in her. She should try to realize that an author must not defend his outlook on the world, but, on the other hand, he must be open to criticism of his writing.

Ernest's mother's constant moaning, criticism, and grumbling, despite his recognition as an author, must have been a significant hurdle in his career. The inability to convince this for him unsympathetic woman of his writing talent could be likened to an author's struggle with a censorship tribunal, a battle that could potentially stifle his creative expression.

Ernest's father, in contrast, presented a different dynamic. While not openly supportive of his son's literary pursuits, he maintained a sense of loyalty. This was evident in a letter dated September 14, 1927, where Ernest sensed his father's disapproval of his books: "I know you don't like the sort of thing I write, but this is the difference in our taste ..."

He was right; the difference is not just about the people but also the attitude towards each person, which can be seen in how biographers judge Hemingway's taste in women. Some of them describe his preference for dark-skinned women. Their descriptions are preoccupied with that Indian girl, Prudy (Prudence) Boulton, who had worked from time to time as a housekeeper at the Hemingway summer home. She was three years younger than Ernest, and in her free time, she hunted for squirrels with her brothers, Billy and Ernest. The story Fathers and Sons vividly illustrates how Prudy, or Trudy as she is known in the story, is connected to Nick's character:

> But there were still many forests then, virgin forest where the trees grew high before there were any branches, and you walked on the brown, clean springy-needled ground with no underground, and it was cool on the hottest days, and they three lay against a trunk of hemlock wider than two beds are long, with the breeze high in the tops and the cool light that came in patches, and Billy said:

"You want Trudy again?"
"You want to?"
"Un huh."
"Come on."
"No, here."
"But Billy—"
"I no mind Billy. He my brother."

Than afterwards they sat, the three of them, listening for a black squirrel that was in the top branches where they could not see it. That Hemingway allowed his Nick Adams to have sex with Trudy becomes more apparent in other scenes:

Than later, it was a long time after and Billy was still away.
"You think we make a baby?" Trudy folded her brown legs together happily and rubbed against him. Something inside Nick had gone a long way away.
"I don't think so," he said.
"Make plenty, baby what the hell."

In her book's preface, *Sweetgrass and Smoke*, the biographer Constance Cappel says that she has been struck by Prudence Boulton's tragic life.

The young girl died in February 1918 in a double

suicide pact with an ex-convict named Richard or Jim Castle. Boulton is buried in an unmarked grave in the Greensky Church cemetery on Susan Lake in northern Michigan.

In 1950, Hemingway raved about a dark-skinned beauty with whom he had spent an evening. She had worn a fur coat and nothing but a fur coat. This woman was Josephine Baker, an American-born French dancer, singer, and actress who was the first African-American woman to star in a major motion picture, Zouzou (1934).

The story is, most probably, not true but would seem to suggest his preference for dark-skinned women.

Like others, Noble Prize-awarded writer Toni Morrison, herself dark-skinned, would have noticed this in his posthumously published novel manuscript, *The Garden of Eden*.

That is why the fantasy of sexual initiation with the Indian maiden, Trudy (Prudy), presents us with greater complexity than simply nostalgia. He, the white youth, grants himself the right to consider an Indian girl as a sexual object but, conversely, threatens an Indian youth with mur-der when he makes advances to a white girl which can be seen in the passage where Trudy's

brother Billy tells of his half-brother's wishes:
"Eddie says he going to come some night sleep
in bed with your sister Dorothy."
"What?"
"He said."
Trudy nodded.
"That's all he want do," she said. Eddie was their
older half brother. He was seventeen.
"If Eddie Gilby ever comes at night and even
speaks to Dorothy, do you know what I'm doing
to him? I'd kill him like this." Nick cocked the
gun and hardly taking aim pulled the trigger,
blowing a hole as big as your hand in the head of
the belly of that half-breed bastard Eddie Gilby.
"Like that. I'd kill him like that."
"He better not come then," Trudy said. She put
her hand in Nick's pocket.
"He better watch out plenty," said Billy.
"He is big bluff," Trudy was exploring with her
hand in Nick's pocket.
"But don't you kill him. You got plenty trouble."

In his Hemingway biography, Kenneth S. Lynn
believes Prudy may have fallen into the habit of putting
an exploring hand in Ernest's pocket while the three of
them sat quietly in the middle of the woods listening for
squirrels in the top branches; she may even have lain on

her back on a bed of pine needles and allowed Ernest to climb on top of her while Billy watched.

Lynn says Hemingway's preference for dark-skinned women would appear to be the truth. If he does not have sources, there is nothing to go on besides this book. One knows that Prudy did exist and that she and her brother spent time with Ernest. Apart from that, nothing else. However, Lynn later says himself: "The truth may lie somewhere in between."

It would appear that, for a time at least, before Prudy started having more serious liaisons with older white boys and mature men like the fellow from Charlevoix with whom she would eventually make a death pact, Ernest thought of her as his girl and that their encounters in the woods were not entirely platonic.

The biographer Carlos Baker, however, sees things differently: "Ernest's fictional accounts of sexual initiation with Prudy Boulton were more likely the product of wishful thinking than of fact."

But even if the stories of Hemingway's sexual awakening and experiences with the Indian girl are not true, it would appear as if he felt very attracted to her. In the story Ten Indians, Nick thinks of the Indian girl Prudy Mitchell.

Here again, there is explicit evidence of racial prejudice and of the low esteem in which white Americans held Indians. It is very clear from the conversation in the coach when the driver, Joe Garner, has to shove drunken Indians, who are blocking the road, to one side and also from this part:

Nick sat between the two boys. The road came out into a clearing.
"Right here was where Pa ran over the skunk."
"It was further on."
"It don't make no difference where it was," Joe said without turning his head." One place is just as good as another to run over a skunk."
"I saw two skunks last night," Nick said.
"Where?"
"Down by the lake. They were looking for dead fish along the beach."
"They were coons, probably," Carl said.
"They were skunks. I guess I know skunks."
"You ought to," Carl said." You got an Indian girl."
"Stop talking that way, Carl," said Mrs. Garner.
"Well, they smell about the same."
Joe Garner laughed.
"You stop laughing, Joe," Mrs. Garner said. "I won't have Carl talk that way."
"Have you got an Indian girl, Nickie," Joe asked.
"No."
"He has too, Pa," Frank said.

"Prudence Mitchell's his girl."
"She's not."
"He goes to see her every day."
"I don't." Nick, sitting between the two boys in the dark, felt hollow and happy inside himself to be teased about Prudence Mitchell.

When Nick finally gets home, his father tells him he has seen Prudence with a youth in the woods, and they were really amusing themselves. Nick enquires further:

"What were they doing?"
"I didn't stay to find out."
"Tell me what they were doing."
"I don't know," his father said." I just heard them threshing around."
"Who was it with her?" Nick asked.
"Frank Washburn."
"Were they – were they –"
"Were they what?"
"Were they happy?"
"I guess so."…
Nick went into his room, undressed, and got into bed. He heard his father moving around in the living room. Nick lay in his bed with his face on the pillow.

'My heart is broken,' he thought. 'If I feel this way, my heart must be broken.'

Prudy Boulton is the first female with whom Ernest Hemingway is associated. Some are convinced that Ernest had his first sexual experience with her. Others are equally convinced that Hemingway's account of his sexual initiation with her is fiction through and through and that this so-called encounter was nothing more to it than a good friendship. But like many readers, Hemingway's widow has always regarded Nick's testimony as a reflection of real-life fact: "Prudy Boulton was the first girl my husband ever pleasured," as she asserts in her autobiography. (She also did not doubt him either when he told her in a London restaurant in 1944 that her legs were just like Prudy's.)

Prudy made the above-mentioned death pact with an ex-convict named Richard Castle. Both took their own lives in February 1918. It was said that Prudy was pregnant. From the reports of his sexual encounters with an Indian girl, it was presumed that Hemingway preferred dark-skinned women. This theory would ostensibly be supported by the manuscript *The Garden of Eden*.

From this and other publications and statements, a whole assortment of fetishes, oedipal castration anxieties, preference for androgynous beings, or homophobic tendencies are attributed to him. It may be that Hemingway's upbringing, especially his mother's twin phobia of bonding him with his sister, led to a disposition to the fetishism of a kind.

I have not found anything in his youth and as a young adult that indicates his preference for black women or mentioned fetishes by concrete evidence. And the preference for older women?

According to all consistent reports, there were girl acquaintances with Grace, Marjorie, or Kate. Schoolgirls, none of whom were dark-skinned, by the way. However, his first great love (the nurse Agnes von Kurowsky in Italy) and his first wife, Hadly, were eight years older than him. But, considering the other circumstances, this does not indicate such a particular preference for him.

I can "put on the table" the assumption that he had a fetish for submissive women. As with the consideration of the role of women in Hemingway's work, evidence of this can be seen in three of his four wives.

The subjugation of the barmaid, Liz, in the story Up in Michigan, is an aspect of this. He describes her as naïve and overcome by infatuation.

In the story, he outlines his idea of masculinity by making it clear to Liz that men and women view sex and love in very different ways. In Nick Adams, the character reminiscent of Hemingway's adulthood appears.

This man has great difficulty having a long and fruitful relationship with a woman who will not or cannot be subservient to him. Three of his wives conformed to this pattern. This man has great difficulty having a long and fruitful relationship with a woman who will not or cannot be, subservient to him. Three of his wives fitted this pattern.

It began with Hadley, who had supported him initially and tolerated her husband flirting with other women in her presence—even to the point where he had practically moved in with Pauline Pfeiffer, who would become his second wife when Hadley could no longer stand it.

The last wife, Mary Walsh, who became his widow, lived up to the image of the faithful wife, although she must have known of Hemingway's reputation and treatment of women, which could not have been any different at the time of their marriage.

The only wife that broke the mold was Martha Gellhorn. Hemingway attributed their divorce to her intense focus on her career as a war correspondent. In 1954, long after their separation, he pondered how she was coping in a world without war.

During the war in 1943, Gellhorn, still married to Hemingway, embarked on a journey that would test their relationship. She left him to travel to Europe, working as a war correspondent. In those times, it was unheard of for a woman to venture into a war zone for her profession. This decision not only bothered Hemingway but also drew disapproval from the American Government.

Post-war, Gellhorn's career soared. She was among the first journalists to report on the Concentration Camp in Dachau, a testament to her courage and dedication. Her work earned her the title of one of the 'great war correspondents', and in 1999, the 'Martha Gellhorn Prize for Journalism' was established in her honor. Her contributions were further recognized in April 2008, when she was one of five journalists to be featured on a special 41-cent stamp by the American Post.

She had been too independent for Hemingway, and he got revenge. In 1943/44, against Hemingway's wish, she traveled alone to Europe, and although she had expressly asked him to accompany her, he had refused but, instead, bombarded her with letters full of tears and longing.When she finally did agree to his wish to return to their Finca home in Cuba, she found him in a terrible state, surrounded by a host of combat drinkers. He had grown a bushy beard and was nasty and aggressive. There was no suggestion of his being happy to see her again. No trace of gratitude that she had returned earlier than expected. However, he knew her greatest wish had been to have remained in Europe for the anticipated invasion on D-Day, the Allied forces' invasion day to the occupied France.

She could have spared herself this return. There was nothing but fights, and even worse, Hemingway humiliated her. While she had been in Europe, where he would not want to go or accompany her, he had (overstepping her) signed a contract with Colliers Weekly, a magazine for which Martha had written and published two hundred and thirty articles between 1938 and 1943. Now, he was flying first class to Europe while she chugged along in the bunk of a Norwegian freight ship transporting divers and dynamite to Europe.

That is how he was and how he grew as a future man. The characters of women and girls I met in *The Nick Adams Stories* he draws from real people: Ernest's sister Ursula, Kate Smith, Marjorie Bump, and Prudy Boulton. These girls knew a different Ernest. In the story Ten Indians, Prudy Boulton breaks Nick's tender heart. In this otherwise so unspoiled Michigan, he seemed so completely innocent. But guilt, as the opposite, lay in waiting, and it made out of him—what would have seemed impossible from this writing—the macho Hemingway who had behaved in such a despicable manner to his wife, Martha Gellhorn. He was one of the boys, the man of men to the marrow.

But the soul of a sincere young man shone through the young Ernest in the image of Nick, who had experienced depression and melancholy in his youth and who had entered adult life weighed down with these experiences. The loss of "life in paradise" is accompanied by melancholy for almost anyone, and it would not have been any different for Ernest. His paradise lasted just a few summers. He was driven out of it, and when he achieved fame, he could never find it again. Later, in the manuscript *East of Eden*, he was frightened of living.

In January 1919, having returned from The First World War in Europe, Hemingway moved to his parent's home in Oak Park. In a made-to-measure uniform but needing a walking stick, he was met by his father and sister, Marceline, at the station in Chicago. He was hoping for a marriage with Agnes von Kurowsky, a nurse he had met in Milan's army hospital. He had enjoyed the company of the Red Cross nurses at the hospital, but Agnes had been his favorite.

She was a tall, dark-haired woman who took all the men, but Hemingway won her favor. He was a war hero and the first American to be heroically injured in Italy. He fell deeply in love with her, but in a letter dated March 1919, she bluntly told him that she was to marry another: "It has come as a surprise, believe me: I am soon to be married."

But that would not have been the worst part of the letter. She began by saying, "I am still very fond of you," but more the feelings "of a mother than a sweetheart."

A disaster. Ernest's war wounds were hardly healed when his heart was broken. He had loved this woman. In March 1919, on the same day he received the letter from Agnes, he wrote to his friend, Bill Horne, expressing his deep feelings for her.

She doesn't love me, Bill. She takes it all back. A "mistake." One of those little mistakes, you know. But Bill, I've loved Ag. She is been my ideal, and Bill, I forgot all about religion and everything else because I had Ag. to worship. All I wanted was Ag. And I'm writing this with a dry mouth and a lump in the old throat, and Bill, I wish you were here to talk to. I hope he's (the man she is going to marry) the best man in the world. Aw, Bill, I can't write about it cause I do love her so damn much.

How it sometimes comes in life, he got his second chance. However, the time had not been right; he had been injured too much, or perhaps a little both. In 1919, he went to pick up his post from the General Store in Horton Bay, and, to his surprise, there was a letter from Agnes. She wrote that her Duke's mother had refused to permit his marriage to an "American adventuress" and that Nicky (his name) had decided to do what his mother said. Throughout the letter, Agnes hinted that she had learned the difference between love and opportunity and that it would be fine if Ernest were her beau again.

Perhaps Hemingway had had a few sleepless nights, but, as far as I know, he never replied. He outlined his reasons why on June 16, 1919, in a letter to Howell C. Jenkins, who had driven ambulances with Ernest:

"I loved her once, and then she gypped me. And I don't blame her. But I set out cauterize out her memory and I burnt it out with a course of booze and other women and now it's gone."

As far as I can judge, only Marjorie was in his life then, and I had already written adequately about their relationship. After Agnes's "rejection," Hemingway set out for Michigan, where he spent 1919/20 around Horton Bay and Petoskey, not with his family at Windemere.

In these two years, he fished extensively on the Upper Peninsula. He was preoccupied with reading and writing and stayed at Windemere when his family left after the usual summer vacation in 1919. His mother threw him out of Windemere in the summer of 1920, and that was the time when he received the letter from Agnes.

Afterward, he was to return to Horton Bay just once, and that was to celebrate his wedding and honeymoon with Hadley Richardson in 1921.

Chapter 7

Michigan was the favorite place where Ernest Hemingway could recover from the wounds of war and the hurtful breakup with Agnes. She had been his first great love and his first real disappointment. Later, it would appear that Hemingway managed to avoid the pain of rejection by ensuring that he met someone new before ending the old relationship. At least, this was the case regarding his wives. However, in 1919, first in Horton Bay and, later, in Petoskey, he comforted himself with Marjorie.

In Horton Bay, he moved in with Liz Dilworth and her husband, Jim, the blacksmith, the house where

Ernest was to celebrate his wedding with Hadley two years later. In the winter of 1919 and 1920, he moved to the Potter's Rooming House, a guesthouse at 602 State Street, Petoskey, where he worked on his first short stories. His stay there is worth mentioning because it was this town where he located his first published novel, *The Torrents of Spring*, in 1925.

The content of that book is bizarre. The character Scripps sets out on the secluded train tracks in the direction of Chicago in driving snow but gets no further than Petoskey. There, he enters "Browns Bean Bar" and consumes hot beans. A no longer young barmaid, Diana, is serving and becomes later his wife. She then spends the day as Ms. Scripps at home. Lucky until she becomes aware of Mandy, the young barmaid from the Beanery, who draws attention to herself with pretentious, stuck-up discussions with Scripps about fiction. Diana tries to get her husband back and subscribes to literary magazines to compete, but she cannot hold on to Scripps. He drops her and turns his attention to the more attractive Mandy.

Petoskey has a pump factory where Scrubs finds labor and meets Yogi. When it began to snow, Yogi and the other workers left Petoskey and the pump factory. Yogi meets two Indians on an open field, and while he tells them about his war experiences, they remain silent. But then one of the Indians says they are war veterans, and he had been a major. The weather improves, and all three return to Petoskey. They then take Yogi to a secret Indian club, but when Yogi admits he is no Native American, all of them are thrown out of the club.

Several unusual characters have gathered in Browns Bean Bar. A naked Indian came in out of the cold late winter night with her baby and was immediately thrown out into the snow, from which she rose and went away. Yogi takes off his clothes and goes after her naked. The two Indians follow, gather Yogi's clothes, and return to Petoskey carrying the bundle.

The whole affair is grotesque in form and content, more of a Dadaistic novel. It is Hemingway's most unusual book, a parody of Sherwood Anderson's bestseller, *Dark Laughter,* published in 1925. What makes this book special is something else: it marks the beginning of a lifelong collaboration between Hemingway and the publishing house Charles Scribner's Sons.

Hemingway had first offered the book to the American publishers Boni and Liveright, but they had rejected it because they were publishing books by Sherwood Anderson.

So, he wrote the book to extradite himself from his obligations to Boni and Liveright, as his first wife Hadley remembers: "Ernest had talked to Scott (F. Scott Fitzgerald) about Scribner's and wanted to go there. He had a commitment to Liveright and wanted to get out of it, so he wrote *The Torrents of Spring,* satirizing their top author, Anderson. I know that Ernest didn't really want to write the book in order to change publishers, but Pauline (his second wife) wanted him to do it, and so he did."

In Petoskey, where Hemingway started his writing career seriously, I found traces of him all over. So, the Little Traverse History Museum, located in an old train station since the 1970s. It consists of three sections. One of them is dedicated to Hemingway and his time in Michigan. There is also a Michigan Hemingway Society in town, which has put up signs in front of all the Hemingway-related buildings and organizes events such as Hemingway weekends. There, I learned that the people in and around Petoskey are not very interested in Hemingway. Only people like me are, who are into literature or have read a lot of Hemingway and are interested in his biography. They come from all over the world. The day before, someone from Argentina had just arrived.

I was able to follow in the footsteps of young Ernest, imagine him leaving Potters House on State Street to walk to the public library or the station to check timetables for future trips and buy the Chicago Tribune. He could be in Brown's Beanery for lunch, or, as people, including me, still do today, could have stood looking into the river from the Bear River Bridge.

What impression did he make on the people in this small town back then? Did he appear to them as a young man who spent his days writing and drinking too much? Who had they seen with no money and hanging around the barbershop telling sailor's yarns and stories? And would his international fame have impressed these people when he became famous, remembering him waiting for schoolgirls to walk them home and spending time with one, Grace Quinlan, or evenings in the kitchen eating popcorn with the other, Marjorie Bump, and telling his best stories to both? What would people who had known him at that time and still remembered him have thought?

It is difficult to say, but possible to imagine that, when he did spend time in Petoskey, he would not have presented a picture of a man in possession of a unique talent as a writer—probably more of one trying to find an identity for himself; of one uncertain of his task in life, who had already experienced too much to be still innocent and likable per se. But it would not have been in keeping with his unique talent if he had not attracted attention.

Later, he would report that during his time in Petoskey, he had spent the whole of autumn and half of winter writing, battling with his emotions, without being able to sell a thing. It was his training ground and apprenticeship. An era of discouraging rejections.

Ernest's first publication, *Three Stories and Ten Poems*, a short novel published in 1923 in a print run of 300 copies, was partially financed by himself. In the following year, 1924, his short story collection, *in our time*, was published in an even smaller print run of 174 copies. The path to *The Old Man and the Sea*, for which he won the Nobel Prize in 1960 or before this fantastic achievement, *For Whom the Bells Tolls*, a novel about people in the Spanish Civil War, had not been smooth. The latter, published in 1940, was sold out in three days in a print run of 75,000 copies. The New York Times called it the "best, deepest, and truest book" that Hemingway had written.

We learn about the genesis of *For Whom the Bell Tolls* in letters from Martha Gellhorn. In 1940, she wrote to the American novelist and poet Hortense Flexner:

I read the last parts of E's book last night. He is like an animal in his writing; he keeps it all in one drawer, close to him, and hides it under other papers. He never willingly shows it and cannot bear to talk about it. It is of course an absolute marvel, far and away the finest thing he has done and probably one of the great war books of always. It is so exact that it becomes truer than life, and yet it is all invented.

To suggest that it's all a figment of the imagination is not entirely true. Hemingway himself said that a good writer can only write about what he has personally experienced. He had first-hand knowledge of war: he had been seriously injured in The First World War and was a war correspondent in the Spanish Civil War.

Martha refers to the plot. Here, it is seen it is not enough to have had lots of experiences; the writer must have the imagination to create the story out of it, which reaches back to early childhood. As I know, Hemingway had always been able "to spin yarns" to tell stories, not only those found in his books. To that extent, Martha had praised Hemingway and was in awe of the book. She wrote in another letter to Hortense Flexner dated August 25, 1940:

> Meantime Scrooby's book is nearly finished: that is to say, really finished, as Scribner's set it up in type the minute, they got their hands on it. We have been reading and correcting galleys and as it is about 200,000 words long that is no joke for anyone. But it is very fine indeed, oh my, what a book. It is all alive, all exciting, all true, and with many discoveries about life and living and death and dying: which in the end is all there is to write about. I am proud of it, and so is Scrooby

Life and death are topics even in Hemingway's very earliest stories, which stretch back to long before his war experiences—even back to his college days and his times in Michigan, where the natural world and related stories influenced him. Conversely, he rarely reflected on his life in Chicago in his work.

In his novel, *To Whom the Bell Tolls*, there is, however, a passage referring to Ernest's experience as a seventeen-year-old of being dropped at the train station by his father on his way to Kansas. In the book, the protagonist, Robert Jordan, had felt more insecure than he'd felt for a long time just as he was about to step onto the train at Red Lodge on his way to school in Billings. Hemingway described it as follows:

… his father had kissed him good-by and said, "May the Lord watch between thee and me while we are absent the one from the other." His father was a very religious man, and he said it simply and sincerely. But his moustache had been moist, and his eyes were damp with emotion, and Robert Jordan had been so embarrassed by all of it, the damp religious sound of the prayer, and by his father kissing him good-by, that he had suddenly felt so much older than his father and sorry for him that he could hardly bear it.

Ernest would probably not have felt all that good being driven by his father to the station, where he would take the train to Kansas before taking up his first job with The Kansas Star. It was an essential newspaper then and one of the best in the Midwest of the United States. It was an excellent address, as the newspaper emphasized training young reporters.

One of the most significant influences on Hemingway's writing style was his mentor, the assistant city editor Pete Wellington. Wellington's insistence on a short, crisp style left a lasting impression on Hemingway. He was eager to make his mark in the writing world and diligently followed the 110 rules outlined in the style sheet for young reporters. *Use short sentences. Use short first paragraphs. Use vigorous English. Be positive, not negative. Eliminate every superfluous word. Don't split verbs. Avoid the use of adjectives, especially such extravagant ones as splendid, gorgeous, grand, magnificent, etc.'*

This emphasis on concise, impactful writing became a hallmark of Hemingway's style. He later said: "These were the best rules I ever learned for the business of writing. No talented person who is honest about his feelings and writing and tries to express things correctly can fail if he sticks to them."

He learned not only from him but also from Gertrude Stein, the American writer of novels, poetry, and plays, followed all the good advice, and was an excellent teacher himself. Everyone who wants to write should know what he said and wrote about writing. And I do not only mean his Iceberg Theory.

Hemingway propagates the form of omission in writing and uses the metaphor of an iceberg, of which only a small part is visible. He argues that everything could be left out, even an ending, and would strengthen the story. Perhaps, but I do not mean this entirely seriously; I was impressed by The Last Good Country (actually an unfinished novel, as I mentioned) because so much is missing. But I second a lot of the theory, which may not surprise me as a poet.

Stories become stronger when they are shorter. When I started writing and had to reduce texts for space or other requirements, I had problems at first. I thought that shortening my text would be incomprehensible and that I would have to explain everything. But I do not have to. On the contrary, much of what I know does not belong in the text but is necessary for me as part of its exposition. It is not an invention by Hemingway but a literary imperative for the fictional narrative.

What makes the Iceberg Theory unique is that it propagates omission per se. "A few things, I have found, are true," Hemingway says. "If you leave out important things or events you know, it strengthens the story. If you leave something out or skip something because you don't know it, the story becomes worthless.

The test of any story is how excellent the stuff is that you, not your publisher, left out."

I recently read a novel I consider one of the best of all time (in my top five). It was excellent in every way from start to finish. However, I realized the author could have left out the ending when I went through it again. She explains something obvious.

She could do that, and it did not interfere with the reading. But the book would have been even stronger without this ending.

When he first came to Kansas, Hemingway stayed with his uncle Tyler, but a month later, he moved in with his old friend, Carl Edgar, whom he had known from his summers in Michigan. Carl said of the fledging reporter: "Hemingway completely immersed himself in the charm and romance of working for a newspaper. He could talk for hours about his work, especially at times when it would have been better to go to bed."

He wrote in short sentences about things he experienced in and around Kansas City. On one occasion, he ran through a crowd of curious bystanders to help a sick man at Union Station. When he saw the man needed help, he took him to a taxi and the hospital. This willingness to help, which would later earn him a medal of bravery when he was prepared to assist injured comrades even though he himself was severely wounded, had always been part of his personality. Hemingway always stepped in to support people in need, and he would take care of them when he could.

His stories range from a newspaper boy's fight to a sad story about a prostitute, to a shoot-out among gangsters, and even to an article drawing attention to the everyday tragedies of a hospital Emergency Room.

He had given up his job at the newspaper when he enlisted.

On his return, much to his parents' disapproval, especially his mother's, he turned to writing. There is nothing unusual about family and community not approving of an emerging writer—and, sometimes, even when successful.

Hemingway knew he could not just write; he had to earn his living otherwise. In October 1919, he paid a short visit to Chicago but could not stand it and returned to Petoskey. He explained it by saying he was not able to write at home. In Petoskey, he worked part-time at the local administration office to cover his basic needs and take Marjorie out or meet friends for a meal from time to time.

But it was not always enough, so he was happy to move when the job offer came up in Toronto.

A wealthy family gave him a large room with a desk where he could work, and for this, he had to escort their disabled son to theatre, concerts, and sporting events. Thanks to the boy's father, he got a job with The

Toronto Star, which would take him back to Europe again. Here are two examples of Hemingway's articles:

Plain and Fancy Killings, $400 Up
Gunman from the United States are being imported to do killings in Ireland. That is an established fact from Associated Press dispatches. According to the underworld gossip in New York and Chicago, every ship that leaves for England carries one or two of these weasels of death bound for where the hunting is good. The underworld says that the gunmen are first shipped to England, where there lose themselves in the waterfronts of cities like Liverpool and then slip over to Ireland.

A free Shave
The true home of the free and the brave is the barber college. Everything is free there. And you have to be brave. If you want to save $5.60 a month on shaves and haircuts, go to the barber, but take your courage with you. For a visit to the barber college requires the cold, naked valor of the man who walks clear-eyed to death. If you don't believe it, go to the beginner's department of the barber's college and offer yourself a free shave. I did.

His mother wrote a letter expressing her relative happiness at his success. However, it still gnawed at her innards that her eldest son had not gone to college and not become a doctor, which would have been fitting in a family that valued the qualification status.

She was probably relieved that her son could earn money with his writing. Nevertheless, it did not improve their relationship. Ernest, indeed, did return to his parent's house in Chicago in May 1920 but almost immediately left again for Horton Bay.

Chapter 8

In July, he visited Windemere with two friends to celebrate his twenty-first birthday. His mother was still unable to accept that Ernest had made writing his profession and accused him of being unemployed. However, he was expected to be in Windemere in summer to take his father's place in his absence. The correspondence between his parents tells that his mother, Grace, had complained about her son from day one.

Finally, an inconsequential event concerned his sisters more than him, which led to him being thrown out of Windemere by his mother. Evidence would suggest she had it premeditated because Ernest got that letter from her, which she must have written beforehand since she would not have had enough time to write such a detailed letter between the quarrel and the expulsion.

This letter displayed Grace's state of mind and the coldness she managed to generate. It is the letter in which she compares a mother's love with a "bank account."

Afterward, until the beginning of October, Ernest lived with Liz and Jim Dilworth. He supported himself by working for them and helping out here and there—otherwise, he spent his time writing. It is said (anew) that Hemingway had his first sexual encounter with a woman during this time and that this experience can be read in his short story, Up in Michigan.

The story created ripples for other reasons: when Marceline, seen by their mother as Ernest's twin, read the story, it almost "turned her stomach." Her disappointment did not derive from her brother's alleged first sexual experience but from the fact that he had used the first names of the Dilworths, Liz and Jim, as his two participants in the encounter—the names of two recognizable, decent people, who were close friends of the Hemingway family.

In a later letter dated August 12, 1930, we see that Hemingway was, at least, conscious of the difficulty he had created: "Have gone over I.O.T. (In Our Time) also the Up In Michigan. I've rewritten it to try and keep it from being libelous but to do so takes all the character away. It clearly refers to two people in a given town, both of them still alive, still living there, and easily identified. If I take the town away, it will lose veracity. But I can leave out enough of the first part to eliminate libel."

The reason why the sex scenes are seen to be so closely bound up with him has probably to do with the fact that the first draft of the story, written in 1921, was written in the first person. Shortly afterward, when re-working it, he inserted the names Liz and Jim—probably because he had married in the meantime. That first draft initiated the autographical speculation and was drafted in the summer of 1921 in Chicago, shortly before his wedding.

It is, however, difficult to understand why he had used the names of good friends he had always felt close to. Not only did he use their names, but he also partly adopted their appearances and patterns of behavior. Today, it does not disturb Jim and Liz (as they, like Hemingway, are no longer with us), but for readers of Up in Michigan, the question remains: why did he do it? Was it intentional? The same question supplies an inconclusive answer when applied to the case of Prudy Boulton or Marjorie Bump.

If Hemingway had not introduced an autographical element in the story's first draft, the question of whether he has forced himself upon the young barmaid against her will would, most likely, never have arisen.

Scholars who have done detailed studies on Hemingway are sure this incident occurred at the bay below Pinehurst Cottage at the end of Lake Street. They are also quite sure that he had never had sex with his great love, Agnes von Kurowsky.

This certainty is based on her farewell letter in which she says her feelings for him are 'more motherly' than those of a 'sweetheart.' They are just as sure that "nothing happened" in Marjorie Bump's or Prudy Boulton's case. According to *The Nick Adams Stories,* these women would have come into question as "first-time" candidates.

The short story, Up in Michigan, is not included in *The Nick Adams Stories*. It was first published in that little volume in Paris in 1923, which was already mentioned, with the title *Three Stories and Ten Poems*. The good thing about being published in Paris was that Liz and Jim Dilworth did not get to see the story. On January 12, 1936, Hemingway wrote a letter stating that the story had not been published and had forgotten the little Paris publication. But apart from that, Up in Michigan was published by Hemingway's publisher, Scribner, as late as 1938.

The story was also removed from his short-story collection, *In Our Time*, published in the USA in 1925. Hemingway was indignant about the fact. In a letter he wrote to John Dos Passos:

They made me take out the Up in Michigan story because the girl got yenced and I sent 'em a swell new Nick story… and better than Up in Michigan although I always liked Up in Mich although some did not. I supposed if it was called Way out in Iowa, Mencken would have published it if the fucking would have been changed to a community corn roast.

The story is simple and almost without plot. The blacksmith, Jim, comes to Horton Bay and purchases the local forge. The young woman who works at Smith's restaurant falls in love with him, but he hardly notices her. One day, he, the restaurant owner Smith, and a third person go on a hunting trip. Liz longs for Jim while he is away. When the hunting party returns, there are drinks to celebrate.

After dinner and a few more drinks, Jim enters the kitchen, where Liz sits on a chair. He embraces and kisses her, strokes her breasts, and whispers: "Come on for a walk;" after that, they go down to the bay.

Jim begins to stroke Liz's body. She is scared and constantly repeats that she does not want it, but she finally capitulates. The end of the story:

The hemlock planks of the dock were hard and splintery and cold, and Jim was heavy on her, and he had hurt her. Liz pushed him; she was so uncomfortable and camped. Jim was asleep. He wouldn't move. She worked out from under him and sat up and straightened her skirt and coat and tried to do something with her hair. Jim was sleeping with his mouth a little open. Liz leaned over and kissed him on the cheek. He was still asleep. She lifted his head a little and shook it. He rolled his head over and swallowed. Liz started to cry. She walked over to the edge of the dock and looked down to the water. There was a mist coming up from the bay. She was cold and miserable, and everything felt gone. She walked back to where Jim was lying and shook him once more to make sure. She was crying.

"Jim," she said. "Jim. Please, Jim."

Jim stirred and curled a little tighter. Liz took off her coat and leaned over, and covered him with it. She tucked it around him neatly and carefully. Then she walked across the dock and up the steep sandy road to go to bed. A cold mist was coming up through the woods from the bay.

The story is crude and without feelings apart from those of the character of Liz. A young, inexperienced woman overcome by love for the older man Jim, who cannot satisfy her romantically or erotically.

She kissed his cheek after he had mercilessly entered her body, and, in the lifeless moments afterward, she confessed her perpetual love for him and tried to get a reaction.

When this reaction didn't come, she felt like her life was over, and she wept bitterly.

The one fascinating aspect of the story is that Hemingway tried to imagine he understood the fantasies of an inexperienced young woman and was capable of describing her conflicting emotions, even in the intense moments when they were coming to a brutal and savage end. How he manages, in a few words, to expose the injured soul of a young woman; how he suggests that Liz understood Jim only wanted her for his sexual gratification; and how he describes the emptiness and feelings of hopelessness when it is over. All of it points to the emergence of the outstanding writer he was to become.

Much later, in 1936, Hemingway expresses an opinion worthy of note at the end of the story: "It is an important story in my work and one that has influenced many people. Callaghan etc. It is not dirty but is very sad. I did not write so well then, especially in dialogues. Much of the dialogue in that story is very wooden. But there on the dock, it suddenly got absolutely right, and it is the point of the whole story and the beginning of all the naturalness I ever got."

This statement is in no way helpful when it comes to the question as to whether it was Ernest who had had sex down there on the planks of the dock. The formulations do not lend clues; otherwise, there is little to suggest that he had. One could imagine Ernest's first encounter with an unwilling and inexperienced young woman, but to say that the story is autobiographical is improbable, considering that Jim is an experienced man. From what I know of Hemingway and his character, this would not have been consistent with his behavior.

It may be probable the first sexual encounter he would have had with a woman could have been with his wife, Hadley. There is no evidence to suggest that he had been with women of openly seductive behavior. Hemingway was 22 years old when he married, and, from the standpoint of nowadays, this would have been late, but a century ago, it was not unusual. This assumption could be, but it conflicts with a letter that Hemingway wrote to Bill Horne after Agnes von Kurowsky had rejected him. Hemingway lamented having left her: "She needs somebody to make love to her. If the right person turns up, you're out of luck."

At this stage, one can assume that Hemingway had a sexual relationship with Agnes, and it would seem as if she was the first woman he had slept with.

What makes Up in Michigan special is not that Hemingway was the man who takes advantage of a young barmaid, nor if it is his first experience of sex—much more critical is the literary perspective of Hemingway, the storyteller. At the end of the story, the woman's point of view and her experiences are central to his writing.

A young man who has allegedly become what others, including his mother, suppose him to be: a young waster without any sense of responsibility who spent his time fishing and hunting, who had little or no interest in his education, and who hung about with mates drinking more than he should. I would imagine that such a man, when writing a story, would be attracted to write from the point of view of the violent seducer and not from the perspective of a sensitive, injured young woman. Hemingway was different. His interest was not only in the ruthless, hormone-driven man but more in the inexperience, feelings, needs, and dreams of the woman. He was sympathetic and caring; otherwise, he could not have written about such matters. A writer writes what he profoundly feels about. I reencounter this sympathetic nature in his dealings with his sister in The Last Good Country and Marjorie in The End of Something.

His writing was not about whether he was sympathetic or admitting to tenderness and sensitivity. More than likely, these feelings were to be concealed in his everyday life. Concessions to tenderness and emotional weakness would have taken him to an area he most certainly did not want to open himself. He would have to appear unmanly and submit himself to the influence of his mother—to be weak and delivered up to her overwhelming domination as his father had been.

From Hemingway's childhood and youth spent fishing and hunting, I can see that exposure to the rawness of nature does not necessarily cloak the sensibility of character; on the contrary, it strengthens it.

He loved just being there, and he enjoyed fishing above all else. He adored the long summers and would feel quite ill in the first weeks of August when he realized the trout fishing season would end in about four weeks. He would worship the looming storms when he would have to cross the lake by boat with his shopping and post. As a biographer wrote, he would have to sit on his newspaper to protect it from the rain and, afterward, have to dry his clothes in front of the open fire—an incomparable pleasure for him.

Chapter 9

After his marriage, apart from short visits, Hemingway seemed to turn his back on Michigan. At first glance, this seems contradictory, but he had wanted to remember his paradise as he had known it and keep his love for it alive as it had been in its original state. He was probably aware there would be no place for the casual love affair he had conducted with his Michigan in his new life.

This Michigan had meant so much to him. It was the only place or thing that helped alleviate and lessen the memory of war. Here in Michigan, he had sensed the need to put pen to paper for the first time. The background to some of his last experiences there, including his fishing trips to the Upper Peninsula, comes to life in the story The Big Two-Hearted River.

Traveling to Michigan's Upper Peninsula by car on the way to St. Ignace, I crossed a suspension bridge where Lake Huron and Lake Michigan meet. Hemingway traveled by train in those days. At this time, he had not yet crossed the beautiful Mackinac Bridge—the third longest bridge in the world nowadays. It was first opened to traffic in 1957.

In Hemingway's days, one still crossed the lakes by ferry. From St. Ignace to Seney was 180 kilometers. However, the Big Two-Hearted River, which gave the story its name, does not flow through Seney.

It is about 50 kilometers away from this place. Hence, those wishing to trace the movements of Hemingway can save themselves a trip to the Big Two-Hearted River. Hemingway gave the story this name because, in his opinion, the name of this river sounded more impressive than the Fox River, where he has the story located. In addition, this river flows through the place mentioned with a railway line. The character, Nick Adams, arrives there by train and heads immediately for the river.

For the story, the name of the river is relatively unimportant, as indeed are the geographical names—even if, because of the story, one of them managed to achieve world fame and the other does not.

Those in charge in the district were proud to have their Big Two-Hearted River receive reference in a Hemingway story. A plaque on the riverbank stated:

The Mighty Two-Hearted River immortalized by
Ernest Hemingway.

Sadly, the plaque was not immortal because it no longer exists.

The Big Two-Hearted River! What an excellent name. I agree with Hemingway: it is far more lyrical than Fox River. The name is Indian in its origin and means twin or double river, indicating that two rivers were close together, flowing into Lake Superior. Settlers inserted the word, heart, in the name. The river, embedded in a serene landscape, bends and curves its way through a colorful landscape and does not convey the feeling that, here, we are dealing with a stream or a great river with two hearts.

There is one small river next to an even smaller one. Perhaps Ojibwa-Indians could have enlightened me on the significance of the *heart* in their Neeshoda Sepee's name, or the first white settlers could have thrown light on the subject.

However, the reader teases out the real meaning of Hemingway's story. It has to do with longing—a yearning for things as they used to be.

The world can stay on the outside, and the character of Nick Adams—in whom Hemingway is easily identifiable—would like his future life to be undisturbed and in harmony with the nature he loves so much.

He is a returnee who suffered from the Great War in Europe. Wounded, he reaches the town of Seney, which in the story has been burned to the ground, like the surrounding forests and countryside. He walks away from it as he did from the war.

He was back to nature, a scorched landscape, and a burned-out soul. Destroyed. Nature is destroyed by fire, and a soul is destroyed by war. Today, we talk of "burnout" and label intense mental trauma or suffering as post-traumatic stress. The atmosphere and mood of the story are conveyed in the following excerpt:

As he smoked, his legs stretched out in front of him, he noticed a grasshopper walk along the ground and up onto his woolen socks. The grasshopper was black. As he walked along the road, climbing, he had started many grasshoppers from the dust. They were all black. They were not the big grasshoppers with yellow and black or red and black wings whirring out from their black wing sheathing as they fly up. These were just ordinary hoppers, but all a sooty black in color. Nick had wondered about them as he walked, without really thinking about them. Now, as he watched that black hopper that was nibbling at the wool of his socks with its four-way lip, he realized that they had all turned black from living in the burned-over land. He wondered how long they would stay that way.

Carefully, he reached his hand down and took hold of the hopper by the wings. He turned him up, all his legs walking in the air, and looked at his jointed belly. Yes, it was black too, iridescent where the back and head were dusty.

"Go on, hopper," Nick said, speaking out loud for the first time. "Fly away somewhere."

The black grasshopper marks a return from war, symbolizing Nick's state of mind and soul in the story. It is a sign of an inferno where everything is burned except for the river, and it is the river that provides him with relief and happiness. When he jumped from the train at Seney, he had expected an intact town but found the destruction; he did a quick turnaround and headed for the bridge without his luggage. *The river was there!*

Of course, the river was still there, but for Nick, it was more a statement of relief, almost as if when in a discourse on Hemingway, the river could be seen to possess healing powers for his broken heart. The severely wounded Hemingway wrote in an unpublished manuscript: And every July, they took him out and broke his heart.

In this manuscript, the narrator vividly portrays a wounded young man, his heart shattered by the horrors of war. His plea to the black grasshopper (go on hopper) as he releases it, is a poignant symbol of his desperate desire to flee from the impending destruction. Yet, the hopper only alights on the next blackened stump.

There is no escape. The anxiety is unrelenting, a constant companion. The only glimmer of salvation is the question: how long would a grasshopper remain black? It's a question that echoes the river's promise of magnificent trout, a promise that seems as futile as the grasshopper's color change.

Ernest Hemingway was 25 years old at the time of writing the story, and this was six years after he had been wounded in an exchange of fire in The First World War. At that time, in the United States and elsewhere, it was taken for granted that it was the duty of every patriotic young man to serve his country in times of war. However, it was not only the *Zeitgeist* that drove Ernest into the army before he reached the appropriate age. How could a young man better express himself as a real man, not a coward like his father? The father's attitude and lack of understanding of Ernest had been problematic since the adolescence of his son, but more difficult still had been his father's total subordination to his wife, who, in the eyes of Ernest, had degraded her husband and his father.

He was just 19 years old when he was confronted with the realities of war and began to realize that "not being a coward" could cost a life and had real bodily pain and suffering upon him.

He wanted to return to a life that, for him, was the life of a proper man: to be back among the forests, the dunes, plantations, lakes, and rivers of Michigan. Ernest longed to be at peace and in harmony with himself and his world.

He yearned to fish, hunt, be alone with himself and his books, and be in touch with the two things that made up life's essence: nature and literature.

In the story The Big Two-Hearted River, Nick's character, Hemingway, gives us insight into why he returned to a landscape ravaged by fire. It probably had a symbolic character for him: a scorched landscape that had lost its innocence to fire and a broken young man who had lost his carefree past to war had much in common. The burned-out and deserted land evoked feelings of destruction, which he had had first-hand experience with. The new freedom he yearned for could only be reborn and revitalized out of the ashes of devastation and despair. His return to the world of nature would have been to the past that no longer existed—to the paradise he had lost.

But there was hope of relief in the symbol of the grasshopper when Hemingway's alter ego, Nick, asks himself how long it would remain black; the question suggests that the effects of a catastrophe do not remain forever.

Further into the story, a sense of contentment sweeps through Nick. He can decide what he wants to eat and where he will sleep, and despite strenuous trekking, he is happy to choose where and when he wants to go next. As can be seen in one of the story's passages, his happiness is almost complete, except for one, typically Hemingway wishes—a book:

He spread the mouth of the sack and looked down in at the two big trout alive in the water. Through the deepening water, Nick waded over to the hollow log. He took the sack off, over his head, the trout flopping as it came out of the water, and hung it so the trout were deep in the water. Then he pulled himself up on the log and sat, the water from his trousers and boots running down into the stream. He laid his rod down, moved along to the shady end of the log, and took the sandwiches out of his pocket. He dipped the sandwiches in the cold water. The current carried away the crumbs. He ate the sandwiches and dipped his hat full of water to drink, the water running out through his hat just ahead of his drinking.

It was cool in the shade, sitting on the log. He took a cigarette out and struck a match to light it. The match sunk into the gray wood, making a tiny furrow. Nick leaned over the side of the log, find a hard place and lit the match. He sat smoking and watching the river …

He wished he had brought something to read. He felt like reading. He did not feel like going on into the swamp. He looked down the river. A big cedar slanted all the way across the stream. Beyond that, the river went into the swamp.

In *The Nick Adams Stories*, we find out why Hemingway wrote so much about Michigan compared to what he had written about Oak Park, Chicago, although he had spent much more time there. Also, in his other works, there is little Oak Park influence but lots of Michigan. Why? The answer is simple and easily deduced from that passage in *The Nick Adams Stories*: he loved nature and because he only wanted to write about things that touched his heart, about things that he could feel powerfully and artfully express in words.

In his writing, every author would only try translating images as they see them. All of these perceived descriptions are present in every person, but the writer's desire and energy breathe flesh into the bones of a picture. If his impressions of Oak Park did not evoke images in the mind of the young Ernest, he had had nothing to write about. Some opinions and voices suggest that he did not choose to write about his time in Oak Park because he would have been obliged to write about family, friends, and their surroundings. There would almost certainly have been a negative spin-off that may have scared him off. Anyway, he did write about it regarding Michigan, which did not scare him off.

The hidden symbolism constantly attributed to Hemingway's work can be traced back to his explanation of what writing should be. Important for him is not only what's on the page in a story but what's not or is hidden between the lines.

It is also worth noting that, for him, there is a significant difference between something not displayed and something that is displayed or evident in writing. It could be that the writer is not entirely in charge of his subject matter and, consequently, leaves something out, or, conversely, the excellent writer deliberately leaves it out to make a difference. In his own words:

A few things I have found to be true. If you leave out important things or events that you know about, the story is strengthened. If you leave or skip something because you do not know it, the story will be worthless. The test of every story is how very good the stuff is that you, not your editors, omit.

Hemingway said that just because you can write short stories does not mean you must explain them. And if a person cannot write, no explanation will help. In other words, the readers should be free to use their imagination when reading what is on the page or hidden between the lines. However, Hemingway did make an exception and added a short explanation to the Big Two-Hearted River story: "A story in this book called 'Big Two-Hearted River' is about a boy coming home beat to the wide from a war. Beat to the wide was an earlier and possibly more severe form of beat since those who had it were unable to comment on this condition and could not suffer that it be mentioned in their presence. So the war, all mention of the war, anything about the war, is omitted. The river was the Fox River, by Seney, Michigan, not the Big Two-Hearted. The change of name was made purposely, not from ignorance nor carelessness but because Big Two-Hearted River is poetry and because there were many Indians, nor did the war appear. As you see, it is very simple and easy to explain."

In the beginning, critics had great difficulty with the story. Perhaps they were not in tune with the author's background. The story was first published in Paris by Ernest Walsh and Ethel Moorhead in their Journal This Quarter in 1925. Nothing happens in the story. Hemingway wrote exclusively about a fishing trip. But this fishing trip helped the returning soldier to heal and forget the wounds that war inflicted on his body and soul, not really the scars on Nick's leg. Hemingway was relieved and happy to be back in Seney. It is one hint at the depth of the story, which only gradually became apparent to critics.

Today, the symbolic elements in the story tend to outweigh all others. For example, the American author and literary critic Malcolm Cowley sees the fishing trip: "… as a flight from a nightmare to reality or from realities that have become nightmare worlds."

Seney is a little place on Highway 28, probably not much bigger than a hundred years ago. In Hemingway's description, the highway crosses the Fox River a little north of the railroad tracks. He saw that "the river was there" from the bridge across it. It is the bridge on Railroad Street. From the bridge, Nick Adams saw clear water gone slightly brown from the stony river bed, and he saw trouts holding themselves still in the current "by tiny movements of their fins."

Hemingway went to Seney and surrounding areas to fish in the summer of 1919 and the late summer of 1920. In a correspondence from August 1 of that year, he noticed the latter journey: "I will be in Seney in a few weeks."

He did not find a scorched landscape but would have it in 1891 when Seney was destroyed by fire. Or in 1895, when the restored town partially again burnt down. Therefore, it is probable that Hemingway, for the story, needed a burned-out town and this landscape for reasons already mentioned. He wrote the story in 1924. From a literary perspective, this is interesting because it was when Hemingway was trying to change his style from that of a reporter to that of an author and a novelist.

Gertrude Stein was the one who encouraged him to change. She thought journalism and literature were opposed to two writing forms. The journalist is more inclined to "inform or report than to create," while she believes it is better "to create than to inform or report merely."

Comparing his texts on his experiences of fishing in an article from The Toronto Star, written in 1920, with his short story The Big Two-Hearted River on the same subject shows how carefully he had followed her instructions.

Hemingway placed great value on the opinion and instruction of Gertrude Stein. In a discussion with her in 1924, he confirmed how "easy" writing, in this way, had become since meeting her. He had gotten to know her shortly after he was sent to Paris as a foreign correspondent for The Toronto Star.

In Hemingway's eyes, Stein was involved, stylistically at least, in The Big Two-Hearted River story. The reasons why this story and its symbolism are not bound up with his war experiences have to do with the fact that, as well as his war trauma in the years 1919 and 1920, he was grappling with his problematic relationship with his mother—that reached its sad climax in 1920 when she threw him out of Windemere then. Furthermore, Agnes, his great love from his time in the field hospital in Italy, had sent him that letter rejecting his declaration of love.

The biographer Kenneth S. Lynn thinks that the metaphor in the Big Two-Hearted River story has to do exclusively with the mother-son's conflict. Lynn bases this assumption on the feelings of happiness that Nick experiences when he builds his tent because he sees it as a home created for himself: "He was in his home where he had made it."

Hemingway wrote The Big Two-Hearted River story four to five years after his fishing trip to Seney. It appears that as well as his war scars, the trip awakened other scars. They had to do with the memory of being thrown out of his parent's home and the complicated, lifelong relationship he had had with his mother. It is imaginable that the homely tent, where he could cuddle up in his sleeping bag, had been a unique home for Hemingway.

It is possible to draw Lynn's conclusions from reading that Nick (Ernest) had left all essential needs behind him and could rejoice in his independence and freedom to pursue the activity he loved most: fishing in one of the most beautiful creeks in Michigan.

However, it is doubtful the writing was only inspired by the disputes with his mother since he did not go camping directly after she "showed him the door" in 1920. The first big fishing trip to Seney was in 1919 and repeated in the late summer of 1920. At that time, he lived alone in Windemere for quite a while.

Lynn's theory doesn't have much going for it. It suggests that Hemingway thought about his home situation and what he had left behind him. But he needed time "to think, write, and do some other things that needed to be done." Lynn's reasoning is too weak to be accepted.

His main argument that the war experiences were not significant is based on the fact that the story does not discuss the war. He held on to his opinion even though Hemingway himself had said that he had deliberately omitted the war descriptions while stating that the story is about a boy coming home from war: "So the war, all mention of the war, anything about the war, is omitted. "

This explanation, published after Hemingway's death, left the biographer, Lynn, no option other than to suggest that these words of Hemingway (as he put to describe him: *the master of manipulation even from the grave*) could be considered reviewers' cliché. He based this opinion on the fact that Hemingway had said nothing about the subject over such a long period.

I want not to condemn Kenneth S. Lynn for his theory but criticize him, considering his theory alone valid. That Hemingway did not write the truth about suffering in war is, perhaps, true. It was his, Hemingway's, opinion that all writers were liars—including him, of course.

Given the adherence to his theories, I describe Kenneth S. Lynn as a scholar who has always held them to be absolute and correct, even when few have spoken in his favor. He would also have believed that Hadley, Hemingway's first wife, is the woman referred to in The End of Something, although it is clear from a Hemingway letter that she is not. Throughout his life, Hemingway had been a storyteller who had often mixed up truth and fiction—the fact that, in itself, proves nothing. He had always said The First World War had taken away from him a lot of sleep, but he had owed it to himself, as a *man*, to overcome his insomnia by his power.

According to him himself, he was in perfect condition. It is to be found in Lynn's biography. He also set up a connection between Hemingway's war experiences and poor physical and mental state, judging from Hemingway's words: "refused to get medical assistance."

And by this, he meant Hemingway's poor condition since the late nineteen forties. Further to this, Lynn added: "From Hemingway's poor condition, it is evident to anyone that he is boasting and talking himself up when he claims he has overcome his insomnia."

Here, in this context, the biographer would claim his statement to be accurate, which he would have depicted as deception in another context.

It is now recognized that traumatic experiences, such as post-traumatic stress, can last a lifetime. It is also acknowledged that it can take years—even decades in some cases—for the sufferer to be in a position to face this condition.

Even from a storyteller like Hemingway, we must take his letter to Malcolm Cowley seriously, dated August 25, 1948, where he stated that he, all in all, was severely injured in the war and a nervous wreck at the end of it.

Post-Traumatic Stress Disorder (PTSD) is a relatively new phenomenon. It was first recognized as a consequence of the war in Vietnam, and it was the war veterans who were first to define it as suffering and an illness and who saw to it that it was included in the official handbook of psychological disturbances in the year 1980. It did not change the large population's perception that would have branded these veterans as weaklings; how much more must this have been the case in earlier wars? Since this effect first appeared and was taken seriously in the eighties, it does not mean that it had not been present in the past.

Ernest Hemingway's drinking problem before the war may have been an indication of his predestination to become an alcoholic. He had begun to drink as a youth, to be precise, since he was fifteen. He even admitted hardly anything gave him more pleasure. That young people enjoy alcohol and, sometimes, drink to excess is nothing new. Nevertheless, drinking like this in younger years is not the only indication of later addiction.

There could be underlying factors that awaken the disposition and evoke dependency. A connection between post-traumatic stress and alcohol addiction is something that cannot easily be ignored or contradicted. Still, I could never know for sure if Hemingway's family difficulties alone were at the root of his addiction. Then, even before his nineteenth birthday, Ernest Hemingway's life took a decisive turn, which could have influenced or been the cause of his behavior in later years. However, his childhood upbringing and his experience of war as a young man present occasion enough for later addiction.

His time in Europe during The First World War and, above all, the physical wounds he suffered were the basis for another form of injury inflicted on him: the injury to his heart caused by his love for Agnes von Kurowsky. Agnes did not acknowledge him "as a man." His love remained unfulfilled, and he fell into the depths of depression. The residue of this experience stayed with him for many years.

His novel, *The Sun Also Rises*, published in 1926 in Paris, gives us an account of Hemingway's time in writing circles in that city in the nineteen twenties and in Spanish Pamplona in 1924. There is the account of a scene where the first-person narrator, the author Jacob Barnes, suffers serious injury on the Italian front during The First World War. He gets to know the nurse and falls in love with her. In his book, *A Farewell to Arms*, published three years later, he again taps into his experience of his unrequited love. The protagonist in the story, Frederic Henry, generally respects war, but he has no intention of dying in the battle: "Not in war. It has nothing to do with me." Henry's world is simple. He concerns himself little with the war.

Passini, another character in the novel, is the exact opposite. He protests vehemently against the war, wants to see it end, and hopes the Austrians will get tired and disappear. Passini is killed in a hand grenade attack, and Henry is injured.

Henry is visited in the hospital by a priest who presents him with a bravery medal. The priest is Don Giuseppe Bianchi, who became friends with Ernest during his stay in Italy. In the novel, Henry is transferred to a hospital in Milan, precisely as Ernest's real life was. Here, he falls in love with the nurse, Catherine, and she responds to his love. Despite Frederic's injury, they make love during her night duty. Catherine becomes pregnant.

On Frederic's release from the hospital, they spend a few hours in a comfortable hotel in Milan. Afterward, Frederic had to return to his regiment and became involved in war negotiations, which resulted in a chaotic mess. He gets into civilian clothes and meets Catherine at Lago Maggiore but must be careful not to be arrested as a deserter. So, he flees across the lake with her into Switzerland. Catherine wants to get married after they settle. There are complications during the birth of their child. A boy is born, but it is tragic—Catherine dies of internal bleeding.

This love story is described in a direct but, at the same time, lyrical language. Hemingway's third wife, Martha Gellhorn, whom he had not known personally then, rejected him initially but changed her mind after reading the book. Hemingway and Gellhorn met for the first time on Christmas in 1936. While visiting Key West, Florida, with her mother and brother, she met

Hemingway one evening at a bar called Sloppy Joe's. "There he sat," she said and described him: "A large, dirty man in untidy, somewhat soiled white shorts and shirt."

Thus, she met the man whom she had written about in a letter in the summer of 1930 the following words: "On the other hand, I think Hemingway is pretty bum from what he did in "In Our Time": the story about skiing is about an ex-beau of mine who used to ski with him. Hemingway makes him inarticulate simply because Hemingway doesn't know how to talk, as a matter of fact that guy can talk in 9 syllable words all night long. So, I'm not impressed. Anyway, Hemingway has affected my style which is really too bad; but there you are."

In the novel *A Farewell to Arms*, she was accosted by feelings she would not have attributed to Hemingway.

In May 1931, she wrote to her former English teacher, Stanley Pennell, at the John Burrows School (he would make a name for himself later): "In the meantime, I will take my code out of Hemingway. Unbelievable, isn't? Do you remember *A Farewell to Arms?* The hero talks to the woman; she is worried about something; and she says: 'You're brave. Nothing ever happens to the brave'. Which is somehow enough—a whole philosophy—a banner—a song—and love."

Chapter 10

As was often the case with Hemingway, this powerful masculine guy could convince by demonstrating his feelings in a tight, precise writing style, which is all the more impressive because of this very style.

There were periods in real life when he lived out the bawdy hero type, but at the same time, his work gives us flashes of insights into his sensitive soul. His love for Agnes, the nurse, might have seemed unusual as she was eight years his senior, but then again, his first wife, Hadley, was also eight years older than him, which, in turn, might lead one to conclude that this had something to do with the complicated relationship he shared with his mother. Towards the end of 1920, Hemingway moved back to Chicago, albeit not with his parents. Here, through their mutual friend, Katy Smith, he got to know Hadley Richardson from St. Louis.

Katy, that future wife of John de Passos, had invited Hadley to Chicago to console and comfort her somewhat after the death of her mother, who had passed away some time previously. Hemingway, now writing stories for The Toronto Star, fell in love with her, and very soon, it became clear that they would marry—even if he did have his doubts about getting married after such a short time of being out of love.

He confidentially informed his friend Bill Smith in a letter where he wrote that he was going slightly mad with the thought that he would no longer be able to go to Michigan on those fishing trips that "he'd always gone on as on a loose foot" and fancy being a free bachelor.

Michigan was his paradise. It was the place he chose to celebrate his marriage to his first wife. He never returned there the same way because of the break and change in life direction his marriage had made. All the happenings and experiences that had turned Michigan into his Garden of Eden were no longer part of his life.

When he did return for the first time in 1940, he had the following to say: "I've always been disappointed in places where I've returned. I have such loving memories of northern Michigan that I didn't want them interrupted."

If, at the beginning, the young Ernest had doubts and was missing his fishing trips with his friends, his love grew more robust and compensated for it.

At their first meeting in Chicago, Hadley was struck not only by Ernest's good looks: "… he was so attractive," but she also carried him away. About it is what Hadley said: "Ernest told someone years later that when I came into the room and was standing in the doorway, he knew that I was the girl he is going to marry."

Interestingly, he chose Horton Bay in Michigan for the wedding reception, not Oak Park, Chicago. It had little to do with the tension within the Hemingway family—but more with his attraction to the area around Horton Bay.

He felt it would be a good time as there would be few people around Horton Bay at the beginning of September. He could celebrate his wedding with people he wanted to have around him.

Even if his return were to celebrate his wedding, he would not have been Ernest Hemingway if he had not taken the opportunity to embark on a fishing trip. He arrived at Walloon Lake on August twenty-eight and immediately set out on a three-day fishing trip to the nearby Sturgeon River.

He invited all his friends to the wedding, and his family made the event the most significant occasion Horton Bay had ever experienced.

Not present, as already mentioned, was his sister Marceline. Although she wrote about the wedding at a later stage, Ursula commented on the inaccuracies in the text: "Marceline couldn't give an accurate description of Ernest's wedding to Hadley because she wasn't there. Carol, Leicester, and I were the only brothers and sisters there."

The wedding could have taken place in Hadley's hometown, St. Louis. A local newspaper had already written about it, but Hemingway would have none of it—he even joked about bringing people to the back-woods. In a letter on his twenty-second birthday, he wrote: "… but we're going to fool them and be married at the Bay in that small, trick church there."

The newly wed had spent their honeymoon in Windemere. Hemingway refers to it in the story, Wedding Day. John Kotesky, a resident, drove the couple down to the lake in his car:

Nick paid John Kotesky five dollars, and Kotesky helped him carry the bags down to the row-boat. They both shook hands with Kotesky and then his Ford went back up along the road. They could hear it for a long time … It was a long row across the lake in the dark. The night was hot and depressing. Neither of them talked much. A few people had spoiled the wedding. Nick rowed hard when they were near shore and shot the boat up on the sandy beach. He pulled it up, and Helen stepped out. Nick kissed her. She kissed him back hard the way he had taught her, with her mouth a little open so their tongues could play with each other. They held tight to each other and then walked up to the cottage. It was dark and long. Nick unlocked the door and then went back to the boat to get the bags. He lit the lamps, and they looked through the cottage together.

It might appear to have been romantic, but the honeymoon was on shaky ground. The weather was terrible, and both caught a cold. On a trip to Petoskey, Hemingway decided to introduce his new wife to friends— among them was Marjorie, which did not go well with Hadley. After two weeks, the young couple were happy to leave their holiday home and return to Chicago.

*

Sadly, the "tiny toy church" is no longer in Horton Bay, but otherwise, the place is not unlike it was when the young writer lived, loved, and married here. As his stories describe, most houses along the road from Boyne City to Charlevoix are still there.

The street is not so heavily frequented, and it is easy to imagine Hemingway traveling on it with one of his sisters or his friend Bill Smith—going to the General Store to buy something or simply sitting on the verandah in front of it.

I could imagine him going to the Fox Inn, one house farther, to collect his friend, Vollie Fox, for a day's fishing or going diagonally across and down Lake Street to Jim and Liz Dilworth at Pinehurst Cottage. He can also be imagined down at the Lake Street pier, settled down with a fishing rod as he used to.

I see myself fully in this magical countryside and finding myself away in a long-ago time named in *The Nick Adams Stories*. I was captured in the immortal sentences of a young man hungry for life and full of ambition to become one of America's most influential writers of the twentieth century.